EASY PIANO

TOP HITS
OF 2021

ISBN 978-1-70515-234-8

Visit Hal Leonard Online at
www.halleonard.com

Contact us:
Hal Leonard
7777 West Bluemound Road
Milwaukee, WI 53213
Email: info@halleonard.com

In Europe, contact:
Hal Leonard Europe Limited
42 Wigmore Street
Marylebone, London, W1U 2RN
Email: info@halleonardeurope.com

In Australia, contact:
Hal Leonard Australia Pty. Ltd.
4 Lentara Court
Cheltenham, Victoria, 3192 Australia
Email: info@halleonard.com.au

CONTENTS

ARCADE

Words and Music by DUNCAN DE MOOR,
WOUTER HARDY, JOEL SJOO
and WILL KNOX

Moderate Pop Ballad

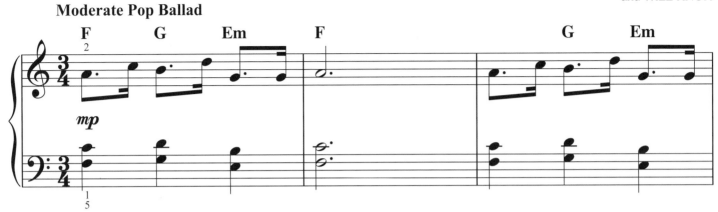

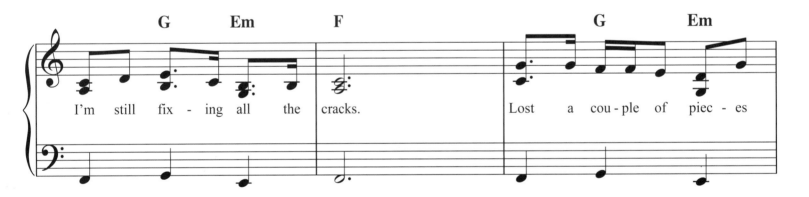

A bro - ken heart is all that's left.

I'm still fix - ing all the cracks. Lost a cou - ple of piec - es

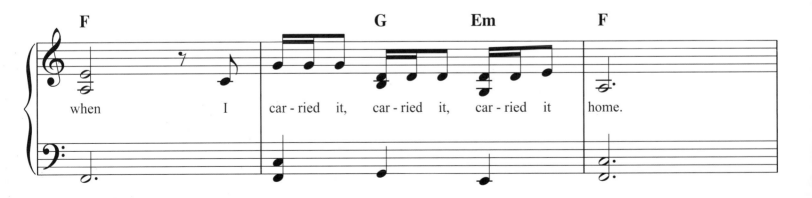

when I car - ried it, car - ried it, car - ried it home.

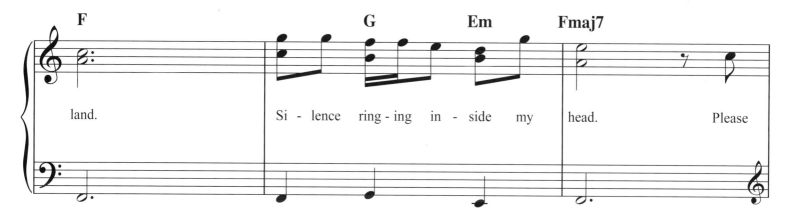

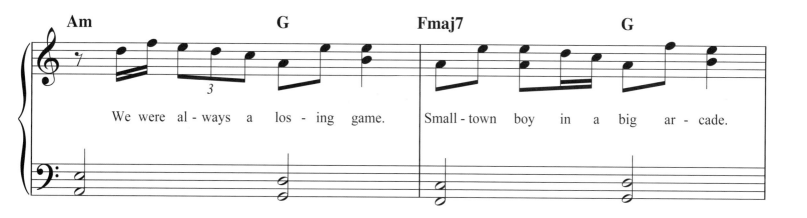

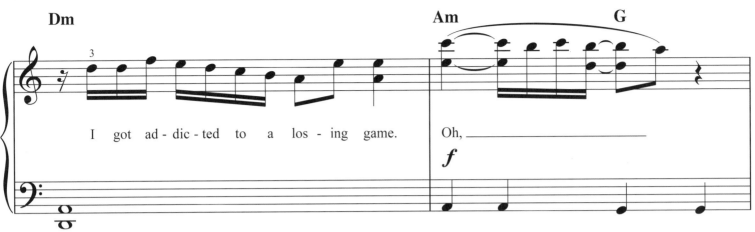

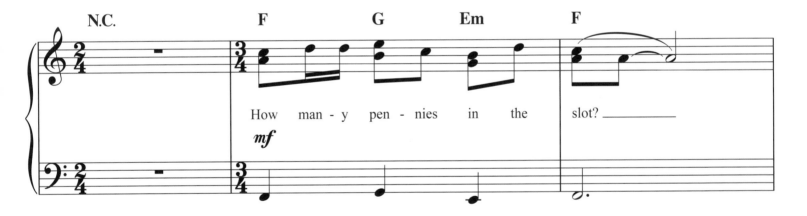

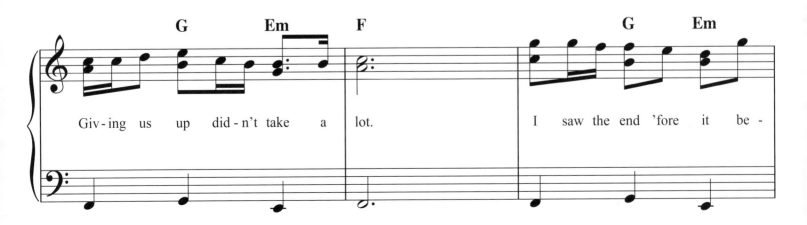

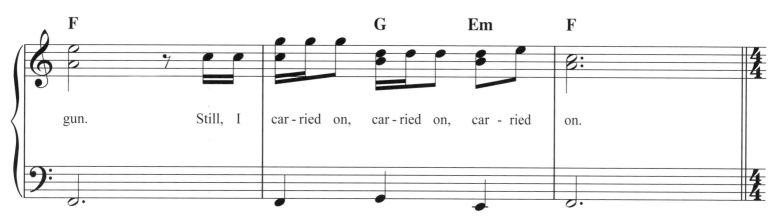

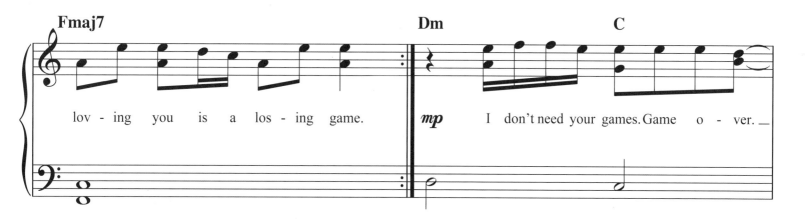

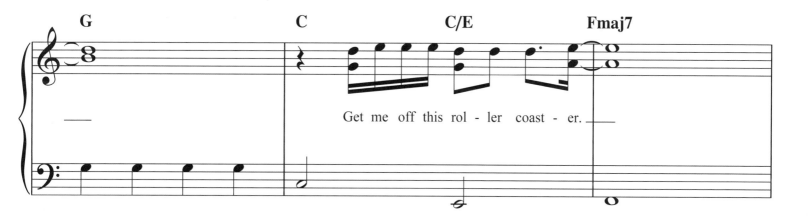

Oh, _____ oh. _____ All I know, all I know: _____

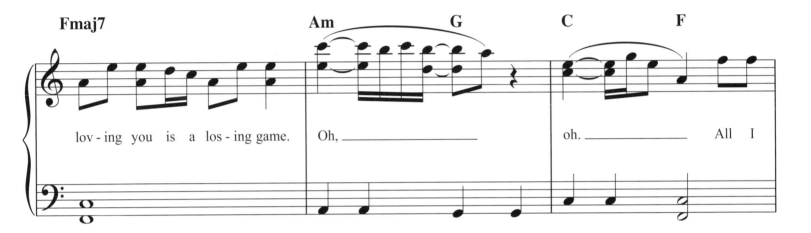

lov-ing you is a los-ing game. Oh, _____ oh. _____ All I

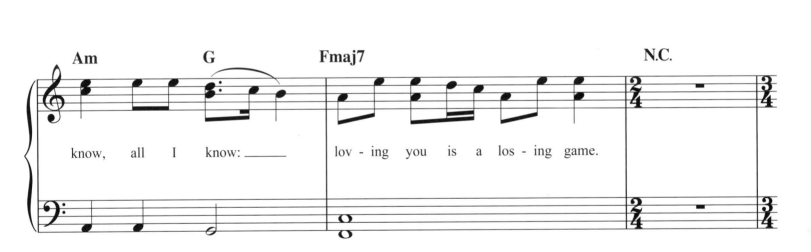

know, all I know: _____ lov-ing you is a los-ing game.

BEGGIN'

Words and Music by BOB GAUDIO
and PEGGY FARINA

Slowly, freely

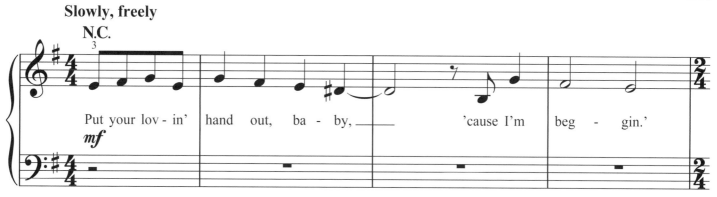

Put your lov-in' hand out, ba-by, ___ 'cause I'm beg - gin.'

Moderately fast, steadily

I'm beg - gin',

beg - gin' you, ___ so put your lov-in' hand ___ out, ba-by.

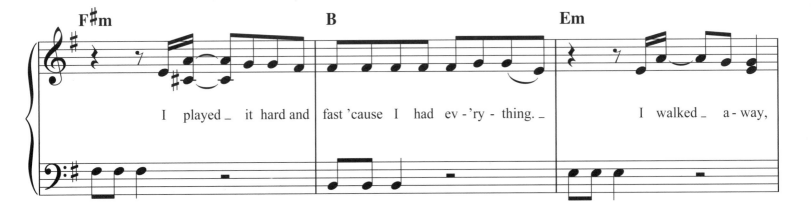

an - y - time I bleed you let me go, yeah, an - y - time I feel you get me, no.

An - y - time I see you let me know, but I plan and see, just let me go, I'm

on my knees when I'm beg - gin', 'cause I don't wan - na lose you.

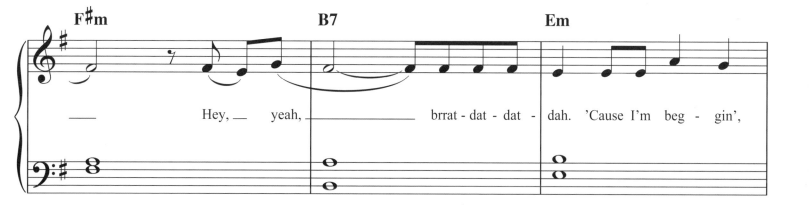

Hey, yeah, brrat - dat - dat - dah. 'Cause I'm beg - gin',

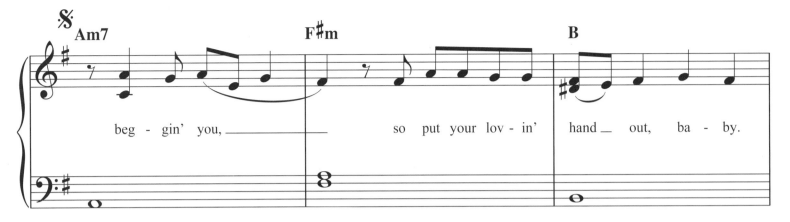

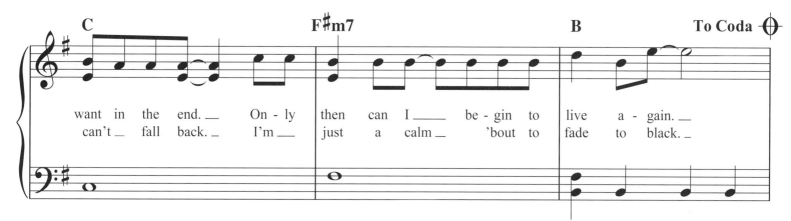

want in the end. ___ On - ly then can I ___ be - gin to live a - gain. ___
can't ___ fall back. ___ I'm ___ just a calm ___ 'bout to fade to black. ___

An emp - ty shell   I used ___ to be.   The shad - ow of my

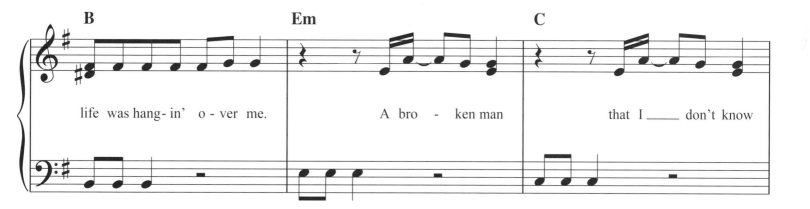

life was hang - in' o - ver me.   A bro - ken man   that I ___ don't know

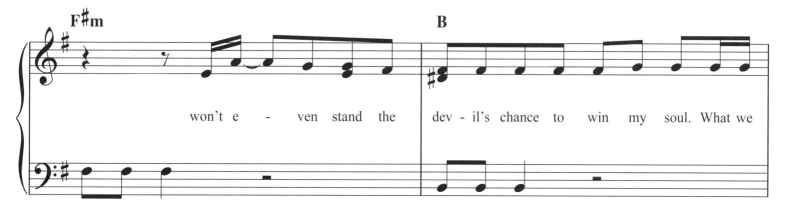

won't e - ven stand the   dev - il's chance to win my soul. What we

do - in'?   What we chas - in'?   Why the   bot - tom?   Why the base - ment?   Why we

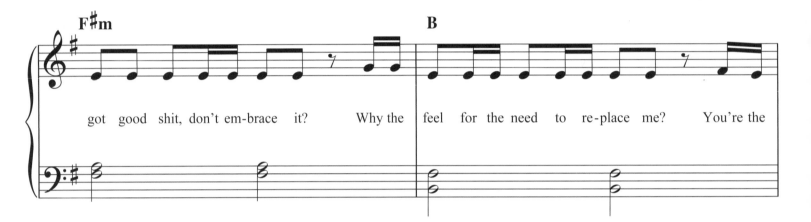

got good shit, don't em-brace it?   Why the   feel   for the need   to re-place me?   You're the

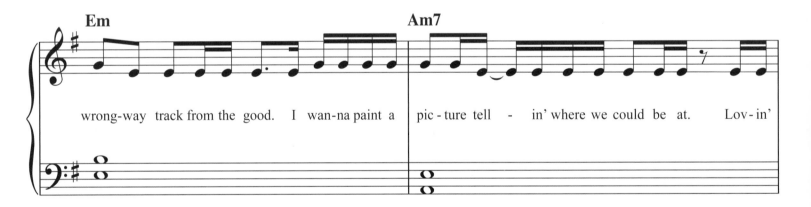

wrong-way track from the good.   I wan-na paint a   pic - ture tell - in' where we could be at.   Lov-in'

heart in the best way it should. You can give it a - way, you have, __ and you took the bait. __ But I

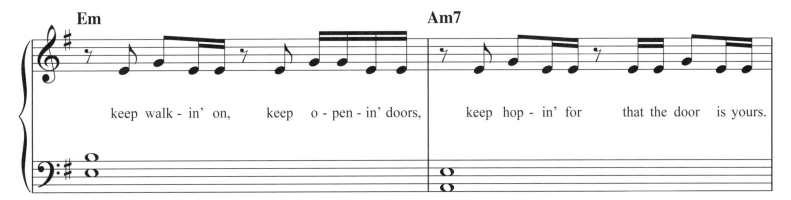

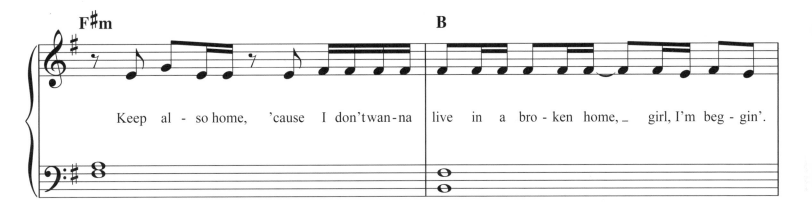

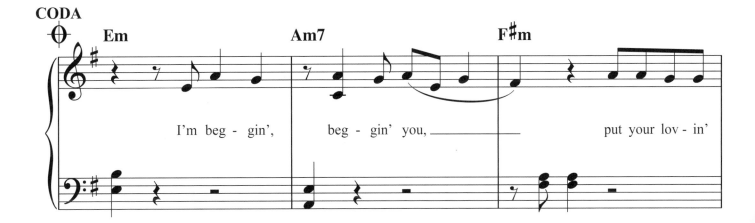

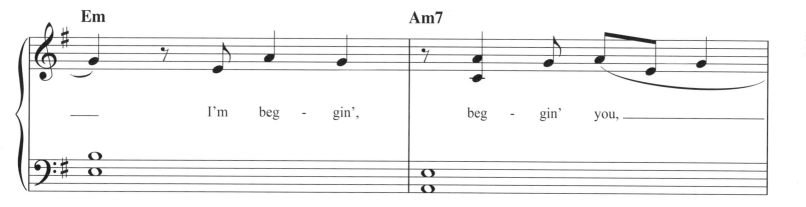

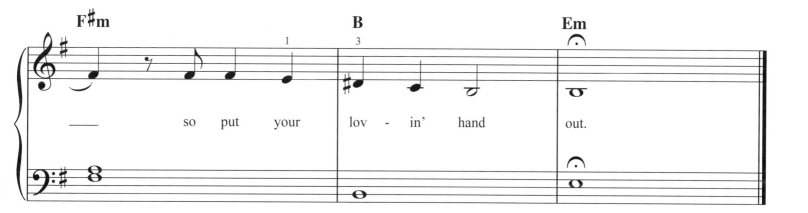

BAD HABITS

Words and Music by ED SHEERAN,
JOHNNY McDAID and FRED GIBSON

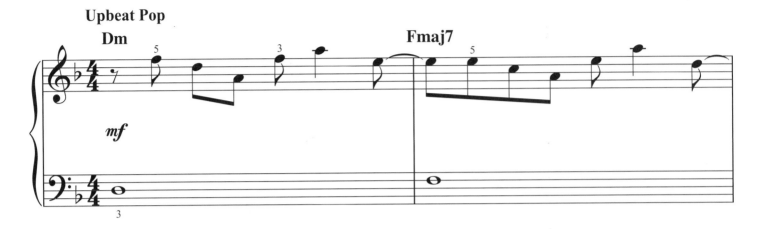

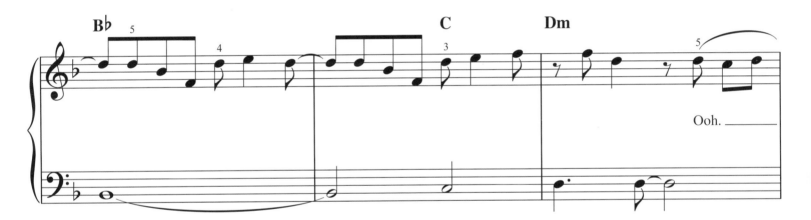

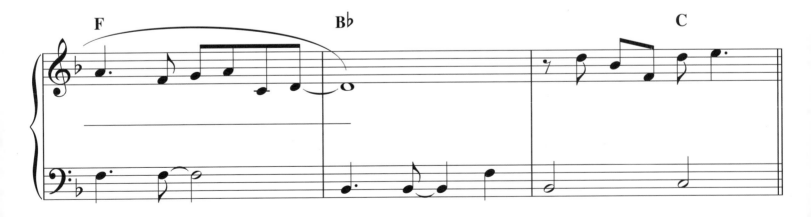

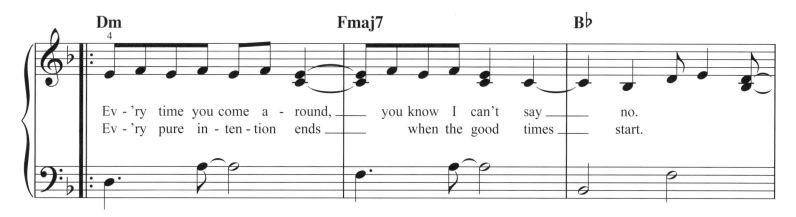

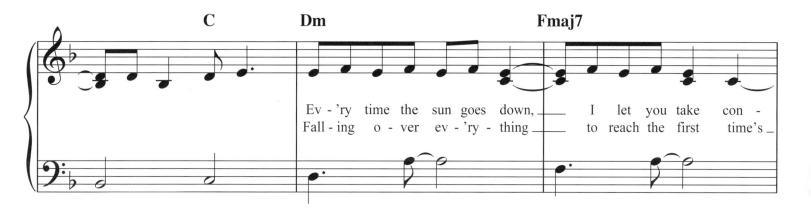

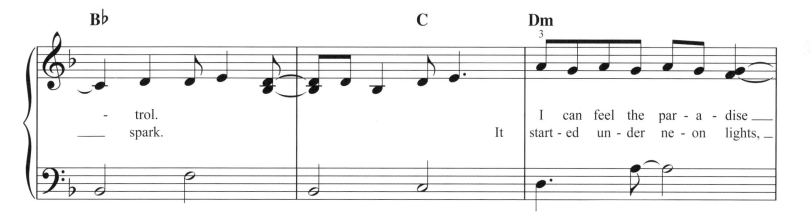

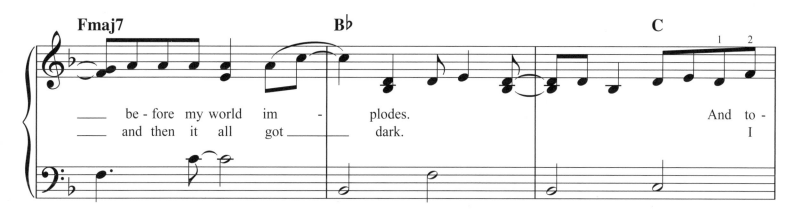

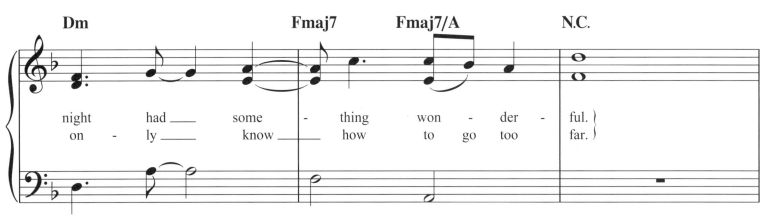

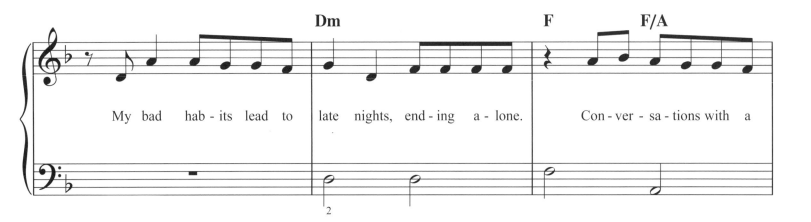

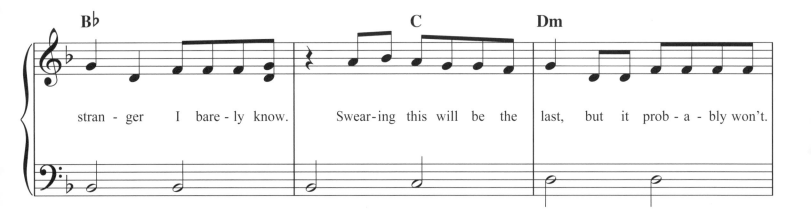

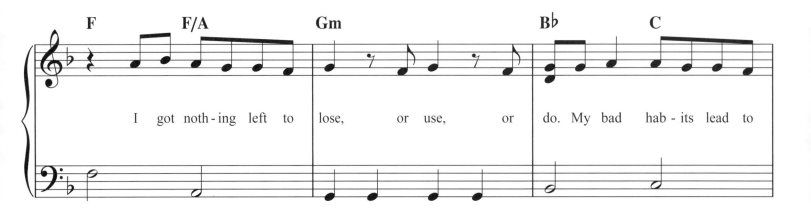

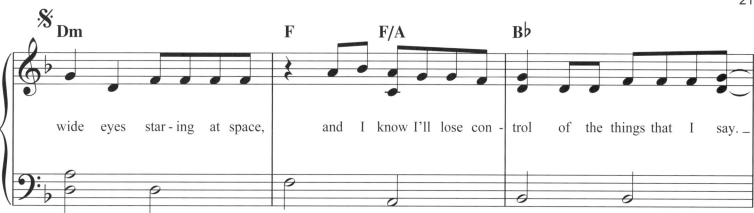

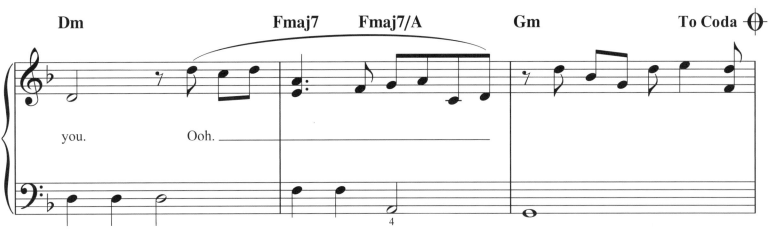

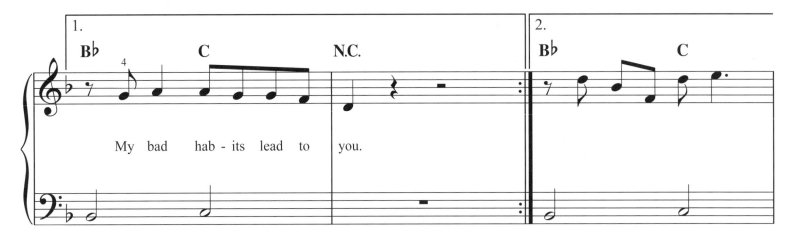

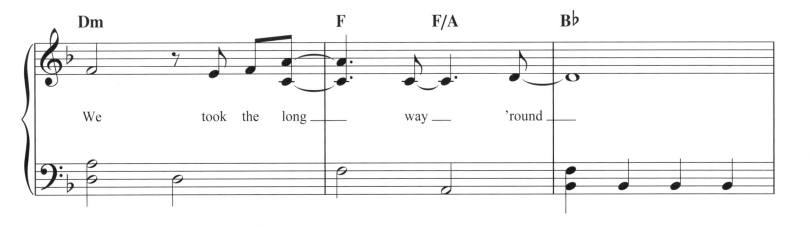

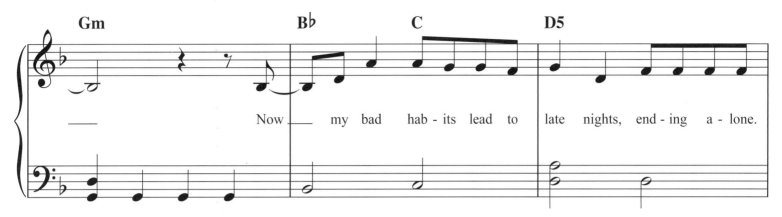

Now ___ my bad hab - its lead to late nights, end - ing a - lone.

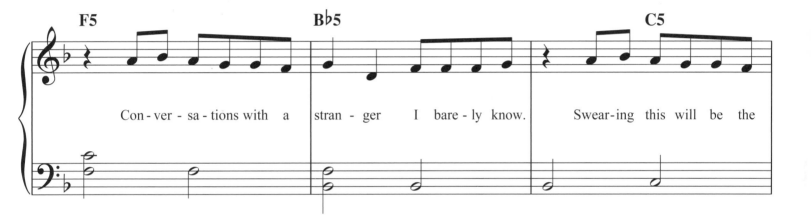

Con - ver - sa - tions with a stran - ger I bare - ly know. Swear - ing this will be the

last, but it prob - a - bly won't. I got noth - ing left to lose, or use, or

do. My bad hab - its lead to

My bad hab - its lead to you.

COVER ME IN SUNSHINE

Words and Music by MAUREEN McDONALD
and AMY ALLEN

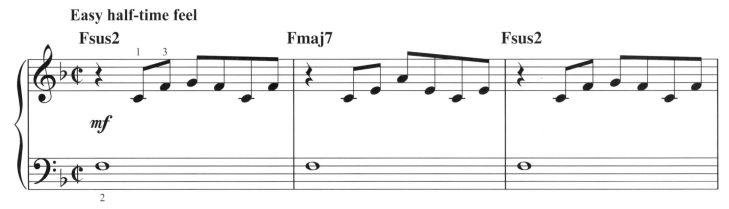

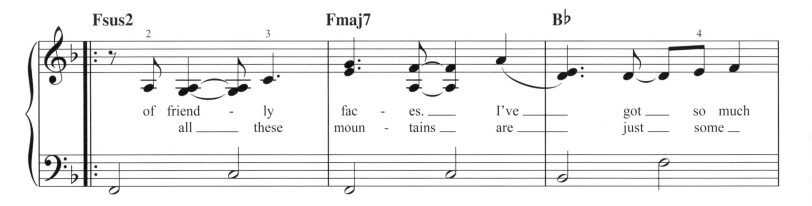

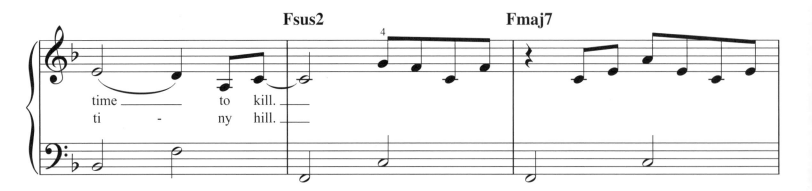

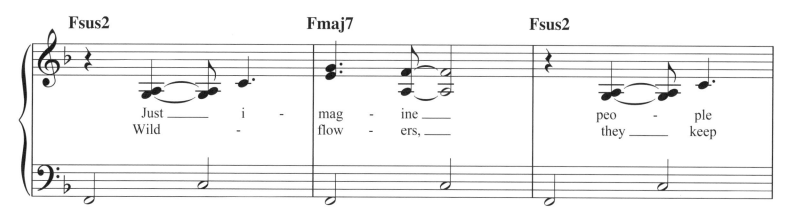

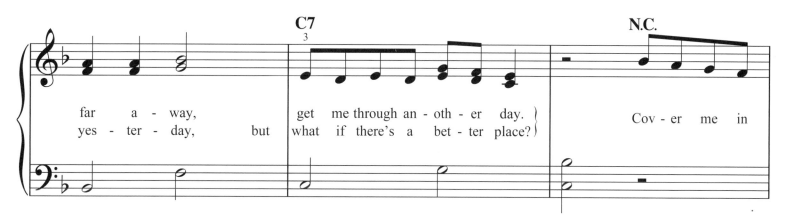

sun - shine.   Show - er   me   with   good   times. _____

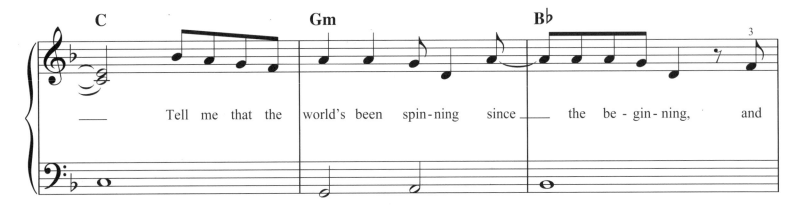

_____ Tell me that the   world's been spin - ning since ____ the be - gin - ning,   and

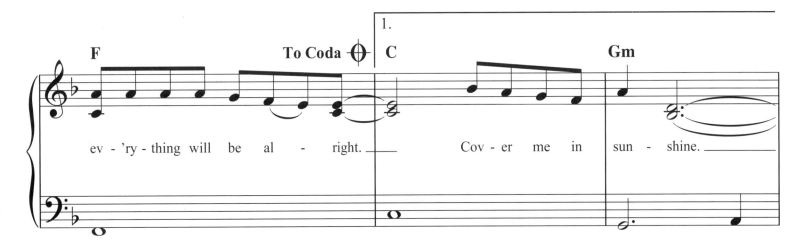

To Coda ⊕ | **1.**

ev - 'ry - thing will be al - right. ____   Cov - er me in   sun - shine. ____

N.C. | **2.**   **D.S. al Coda**

_____   From __ a   dis - tance, __   ____ Cov - er me in

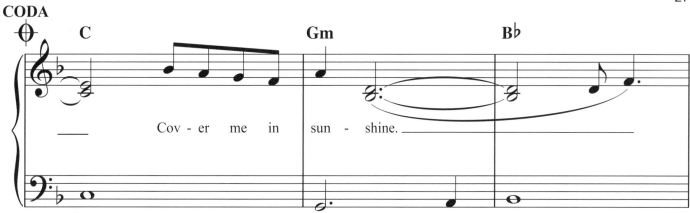

CODA

C   Gm   Bb

Cov - er me in sun - shine.

C7   Gm

La   la   la.

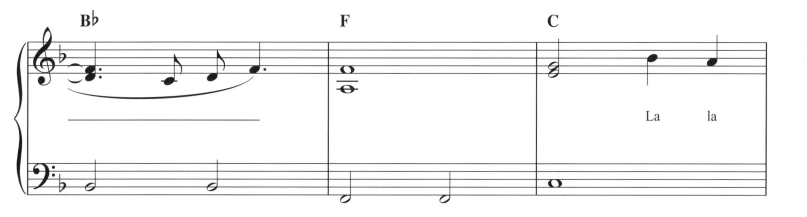

Bb   F   C

La   la

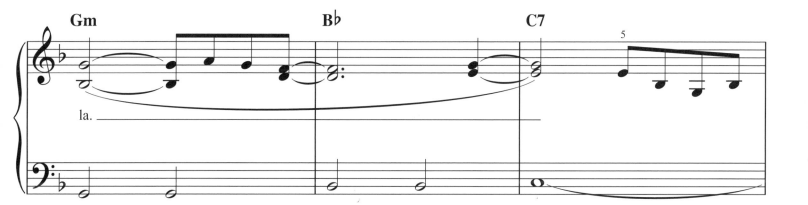

Gm   Bb   C7

la.

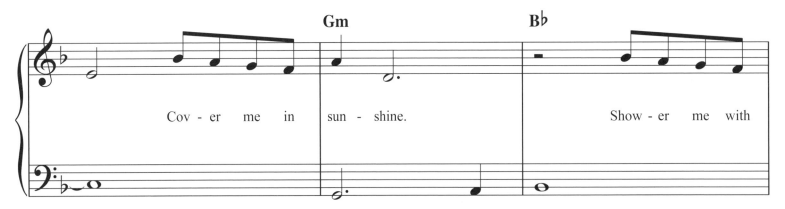

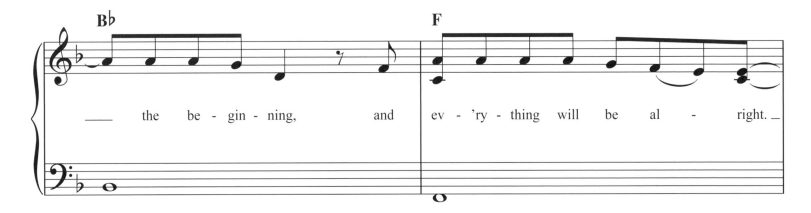

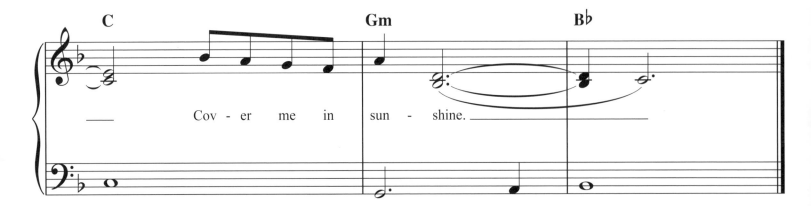

DEJA VU

Words and Music by OLIVIA RODRIGO,
DANIEL NIGRO, JACK ANTONOFF,
TAYLOR SWIFT and ANNIE CLARK

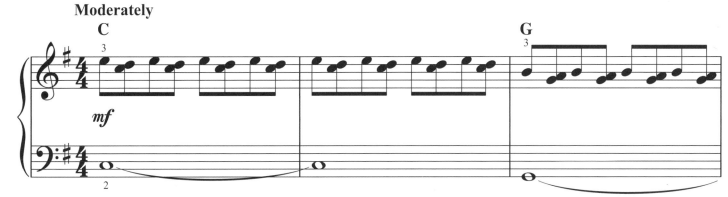

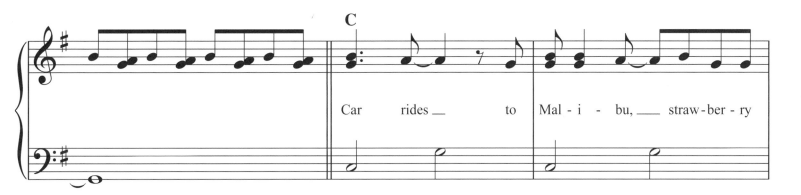

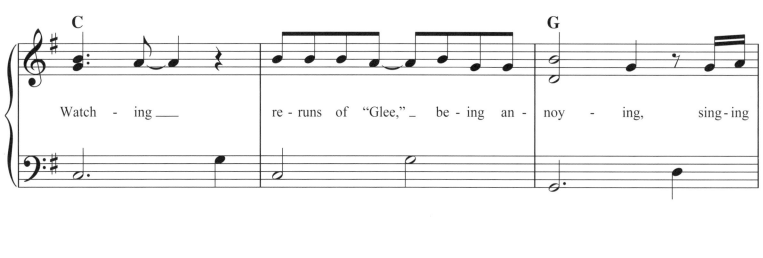

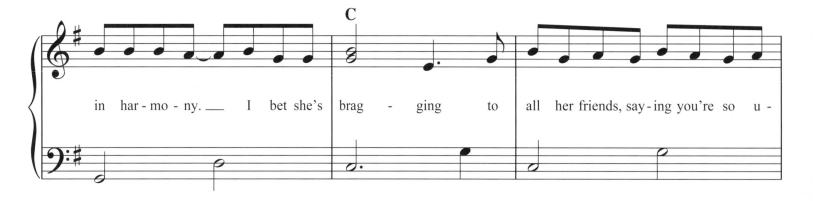

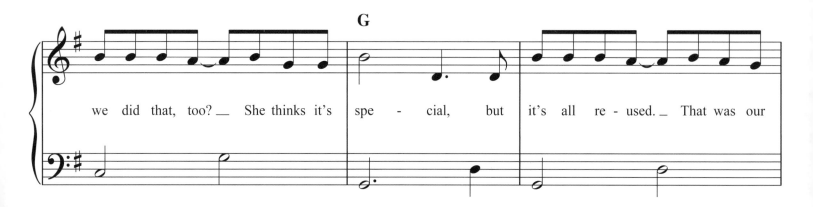

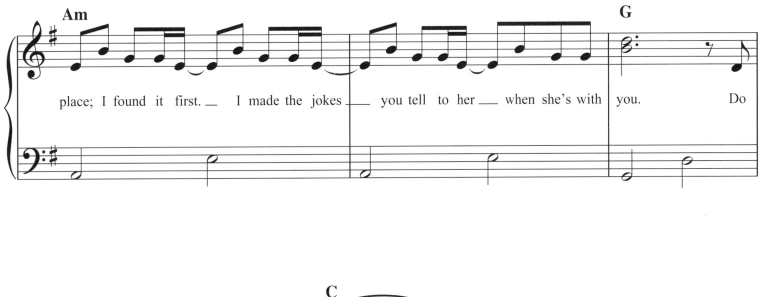

place; I found it first. __ I made the jokes __ you tell to her __ when she's with you. Do

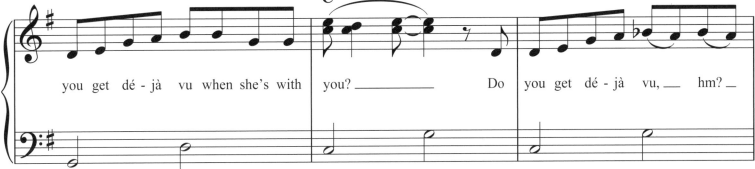

you get dé - jà vu when she's with you? _____ Do you get dé - jà vu, __ hm? __

Do you get dé - jà vu, huh? Do

Do you call her, __ al - most

say my name? _ 'Cause let's be hon - est, we kind - a do sound the same. _ An - oth - er

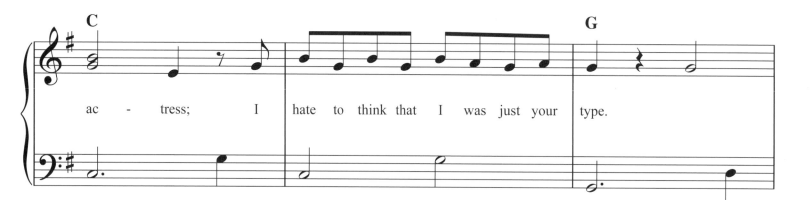

ac - tress; I hate to think that I was just your type.

I bet that she knows Bil - ly Joel 'cause you played her "Up - town Girl." You're

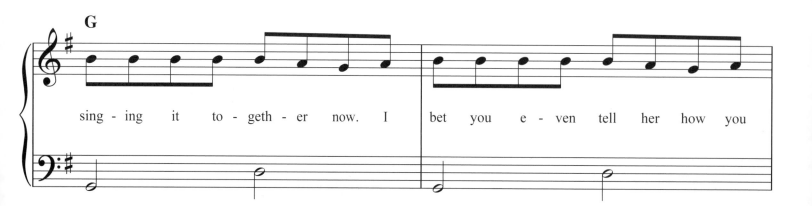

sing - ing it to - geth - er now. I bet you e - ven tell her how you

love her in be-tween the cho-rus and the verse.

So, when you gon-na tell her that we did that, too? __ She thinks it's

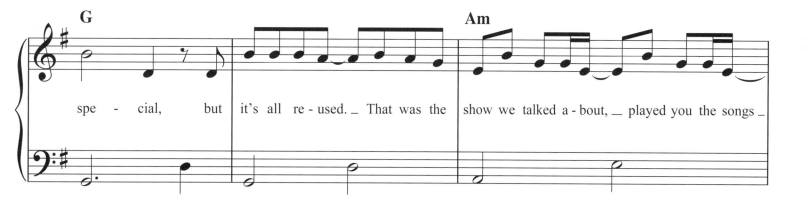

spe - cial, but it's all re-used. __ That was the show we talked a-bout, __ played you the songs __

__ she's sing-ing now __ when she's with you. Do you get dé-jà vu when she's with

you? _____ Do you get dé - jà vu? __ Oh. __ Do

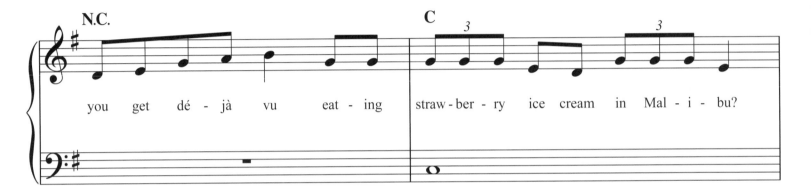

you get dé - jà vu eat - ing straw - ber - ry ice cream in Mal - i - bu?

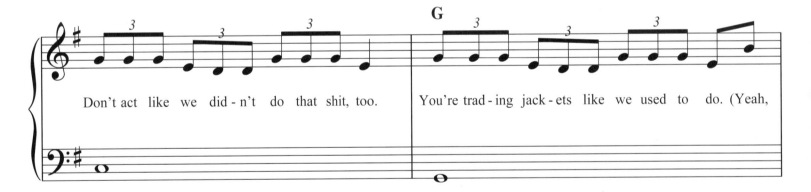

Don't act like we did - n't do that shit, too. You're trad - ing jack - ets like we used to do. (Yeah,

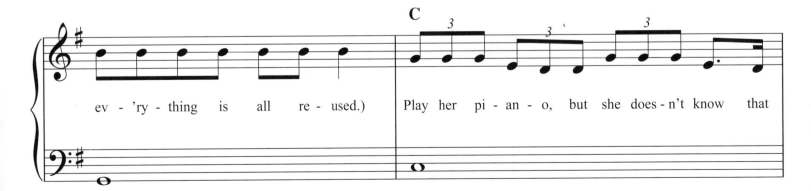

ev - 'ry - thing is all re - used.) Play her pi - an - o, but she does - n't know that

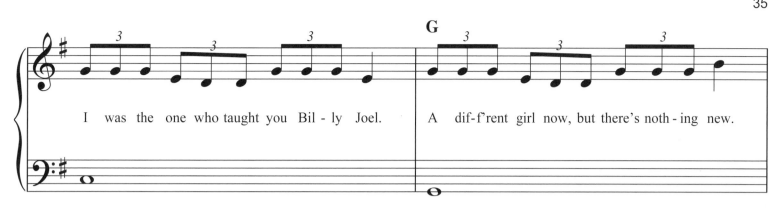

I was the one who taught you Bil - ly Joel. A dif-f'rent girl now, but there's noth - ing new.

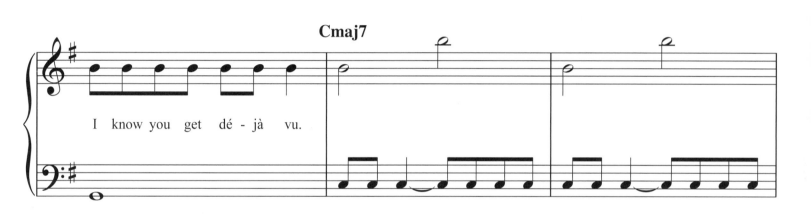

I know you get dé - jà vu.

I know you get dé - jà vu.

I know you get dé - jà vu.

FOLLOW YOU

Words and Music by DAN REYNOLDS,
WAYNE SERMON, BEN McKEE,
DANIEL PLATZMAN, ELLEY DUHÉ,
JOEL LITTLE and FRANSICSA HALL

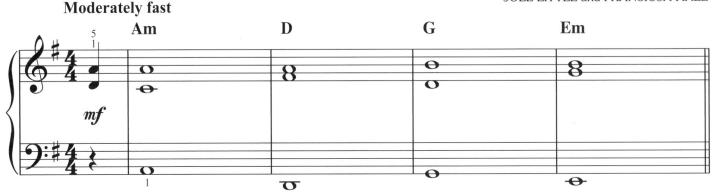

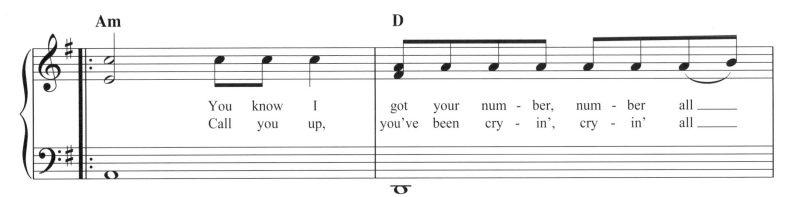

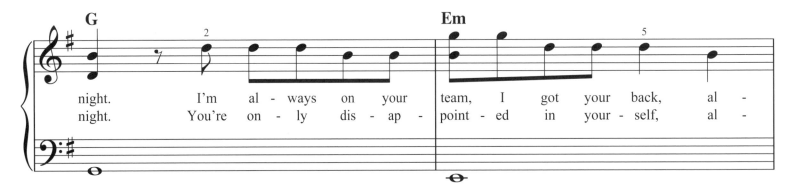

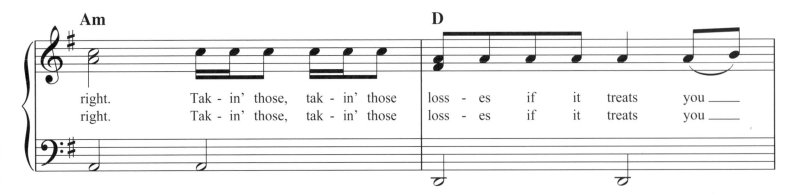

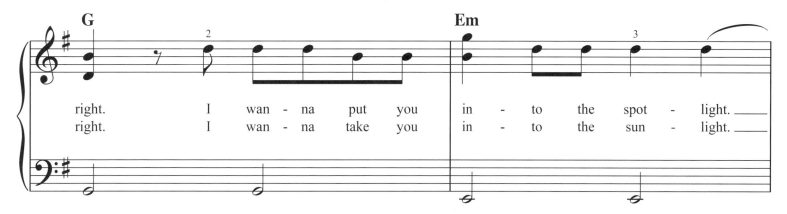

right. I wan - na put you in - to the spot - light. ____
right. I wan - na take you in - to the sun - light. ____

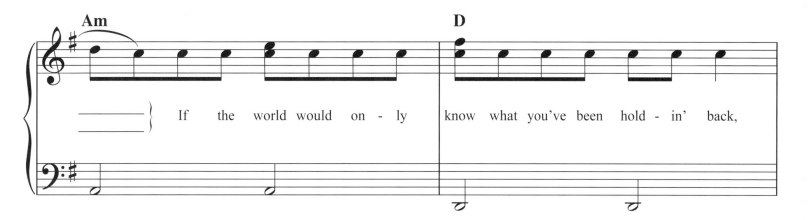

____ { If the world would on - ly know what you've been hold - in' back,

heart at - tacks ev - 'ry night. Oh, you know it's not right. I will fol - low you way

down wher - ev - er you may go. I'll fol - low you way down to your deep - est

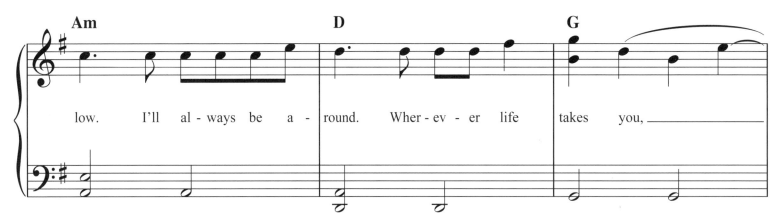

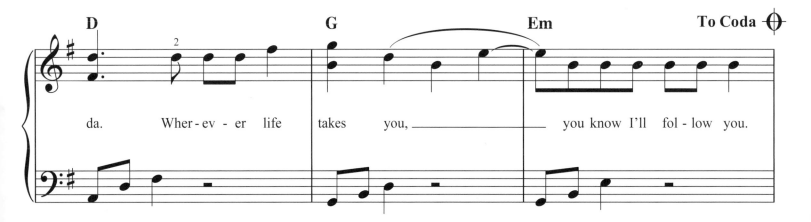

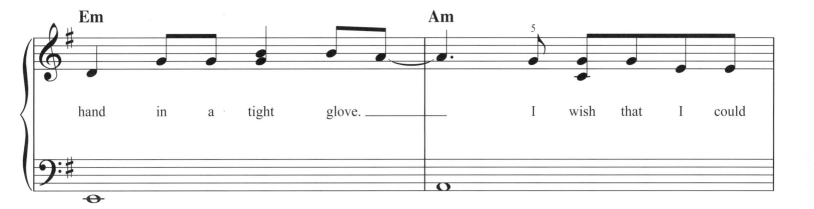

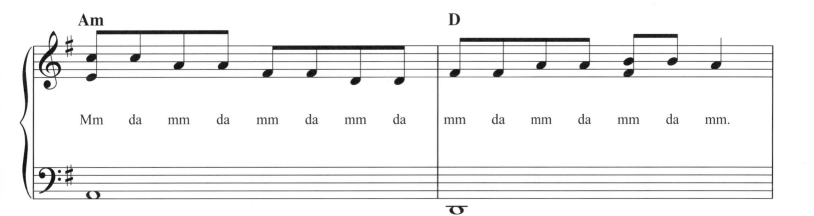

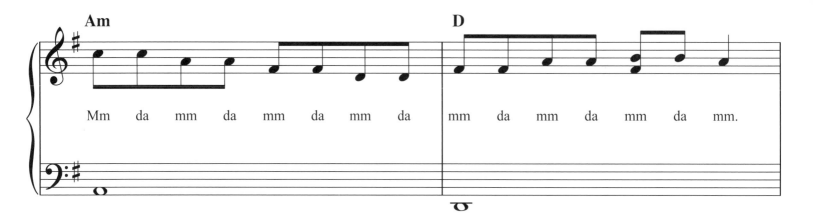

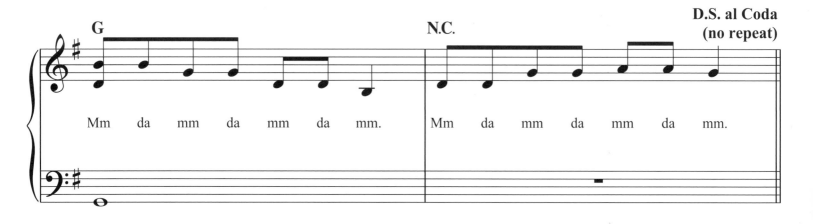

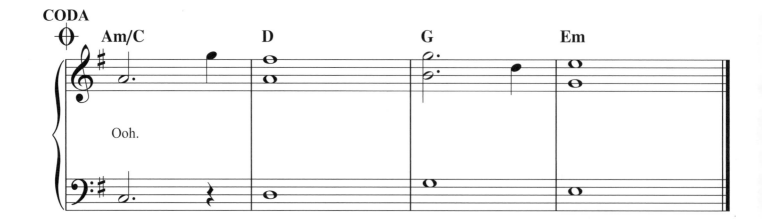

THE GOOD ONES

Words and Music by GABBY BARRETT,
ZACHARY KALE, EMILY FOX LANDIS
and JAMES McCORMICK

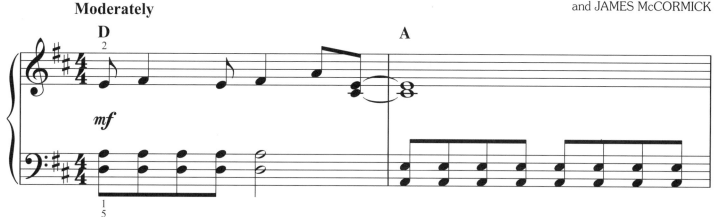

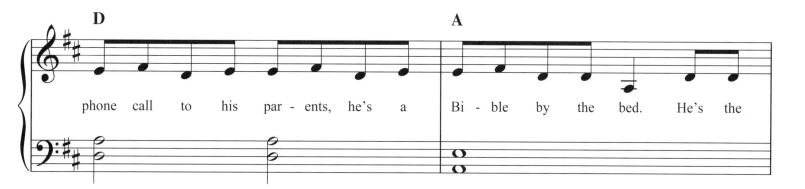

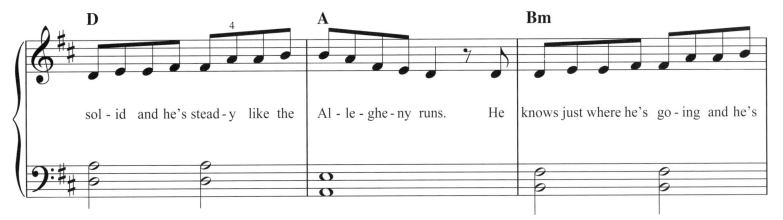

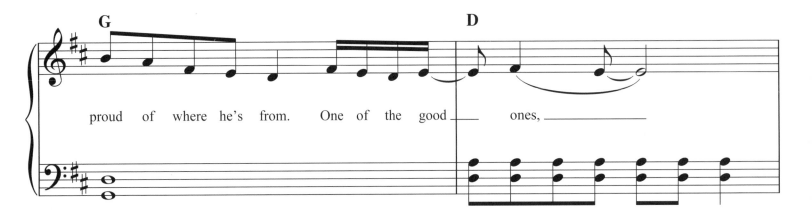

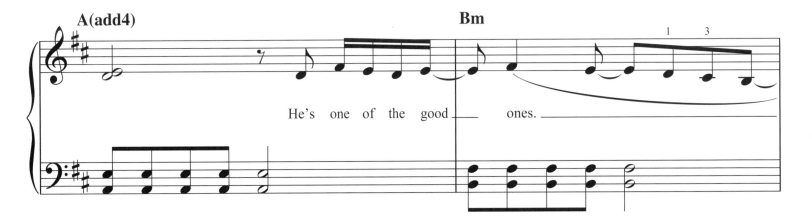

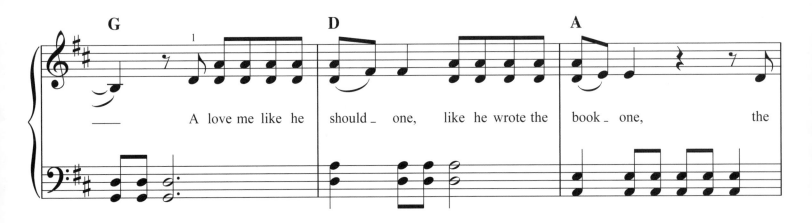

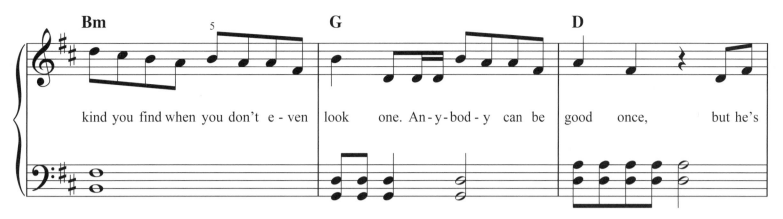

kind you find when you don't e - ven look one. An - y - bod - y can be good once, but he's

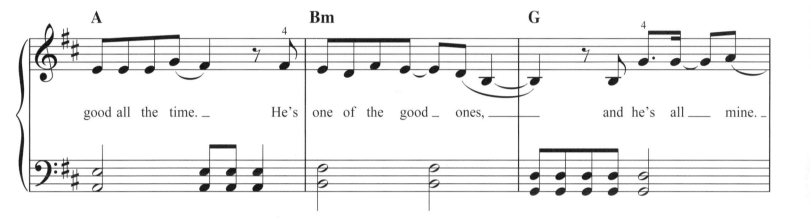

good all the time. _____ He's one of the good _ ones, _____ and he's all ___ mine. _

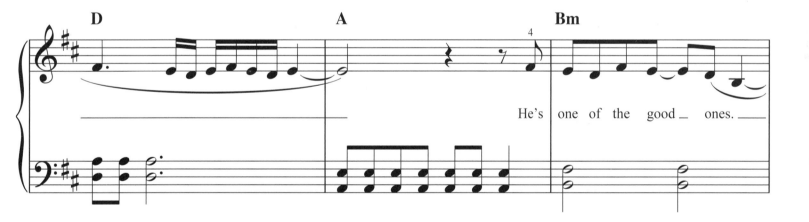

_____ He's one of the good _ ones. _____

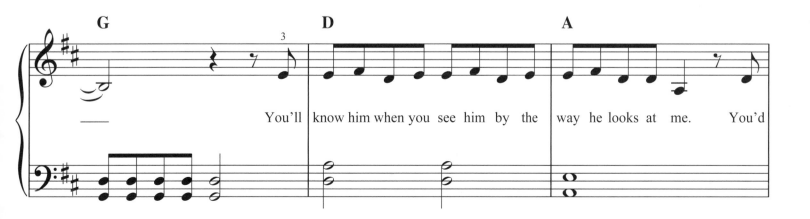

_ You'll know him when you see him by the way he looks at me. You'd

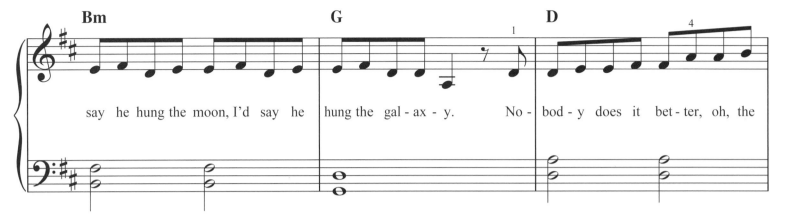

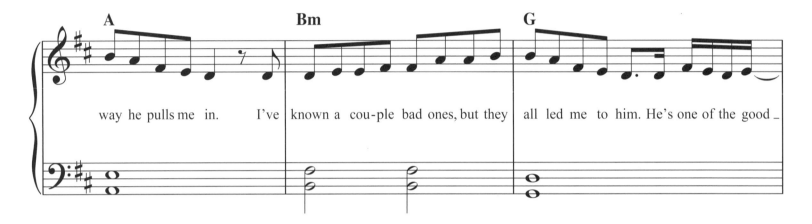

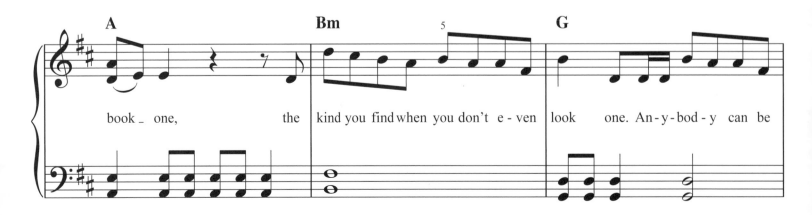

good once, but he's good all the time. __ He's one of the good __ ones, _____

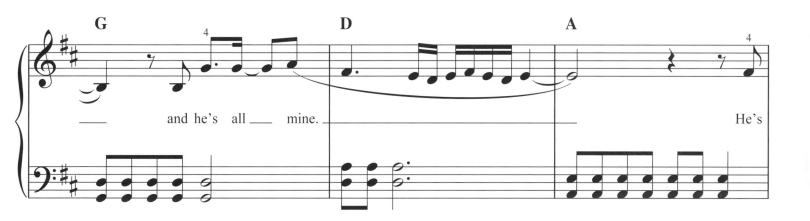

__ and he's all __ mine. _____ He's

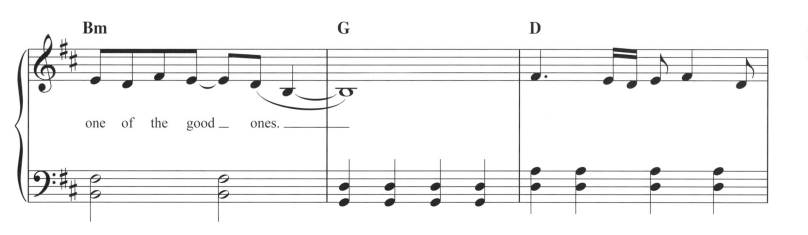

one of the good __ ones. _____

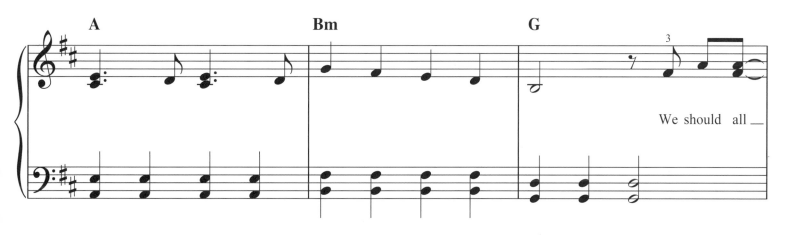

We should all __

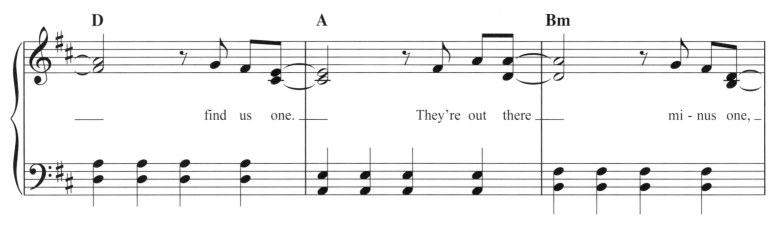

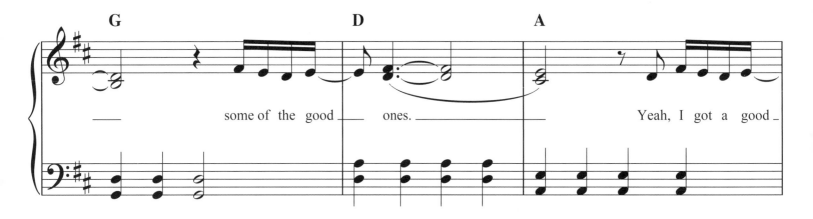

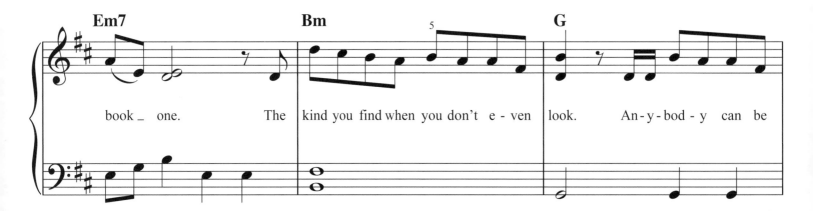

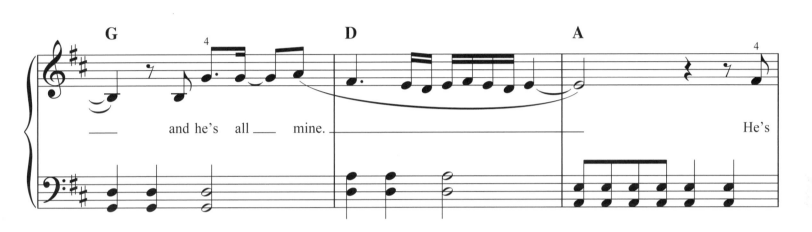

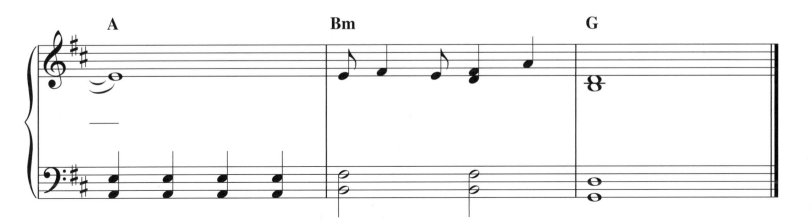

GOOD 4 U

Words and Music by OLIVIA RODRIGO,
DANIEL NIGRO, HAYLEY WILLIAMS
and JOSH FARRO

Driving Pop Rock

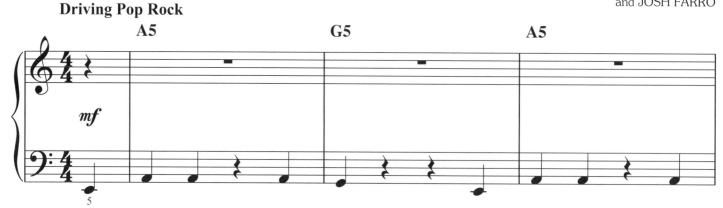

(Ah.) Well, good for you, I guess you moved on real - ly eas - i - ly.

You found a new girl and it on - ly took a cou - ple weeks. Re - mem - ber when you said that

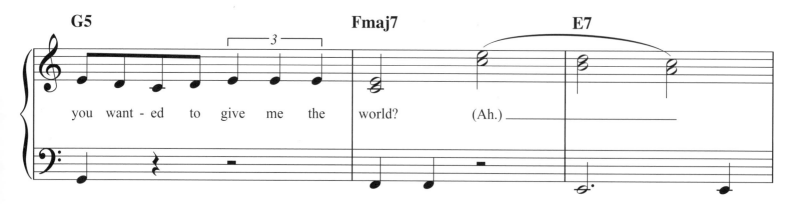

you want - ed to give me the world? (Ah.)

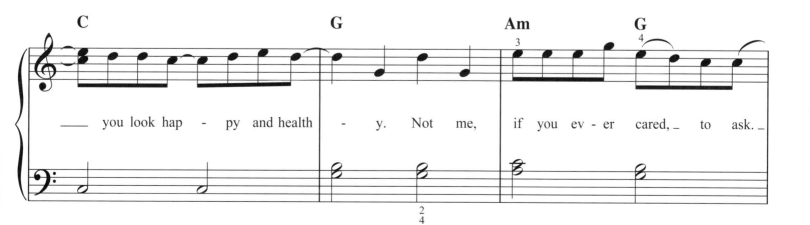

Good for you, ____ you're do - ing great out there with - out me, ba - by.

God, I wish that I could do that. ____ I've lost my mind, _ I've spent the night _

____ cry - ing on the floor of my ___ bath - room. But you're so un - af - fect -

- ed, I real - ly don't get it, but I guess good for you. ____

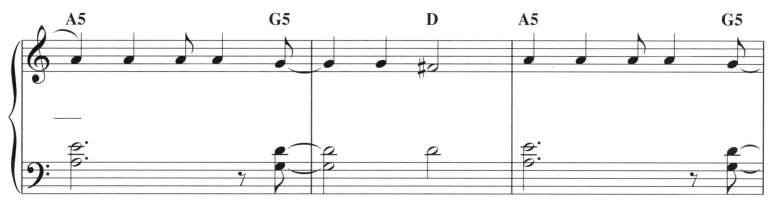

Well, good for you, I guess you're get- ting ev-'ry-thing you want.

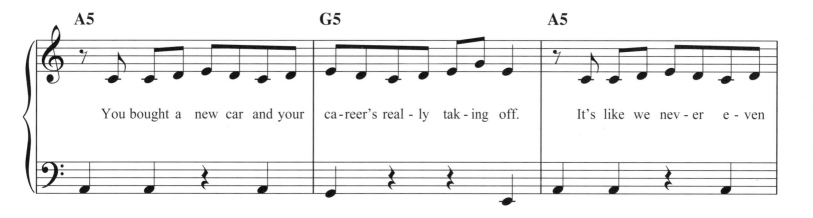

You bought a new car and your ca- reer's real- ly tak- ing off. It's like we nev- er e- ven

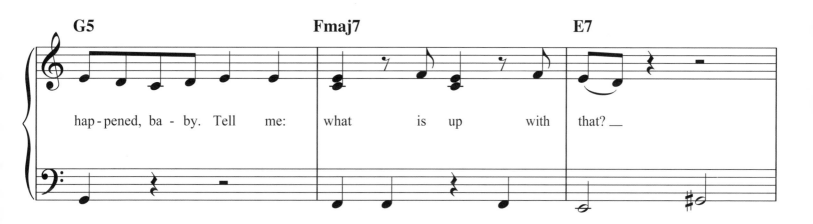

hap- pened, ba- by. Tell me: what is up with that? __

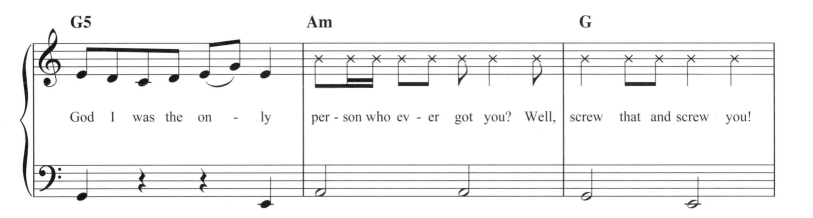

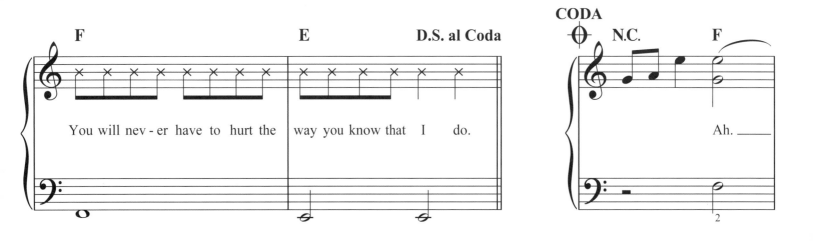

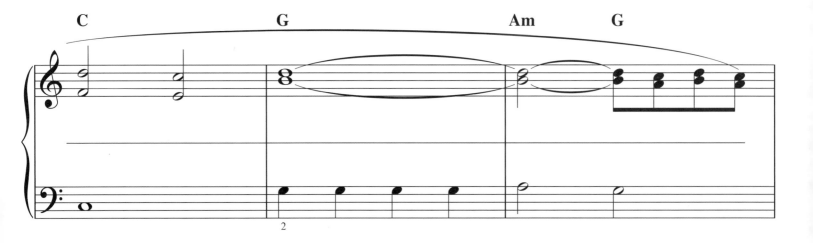

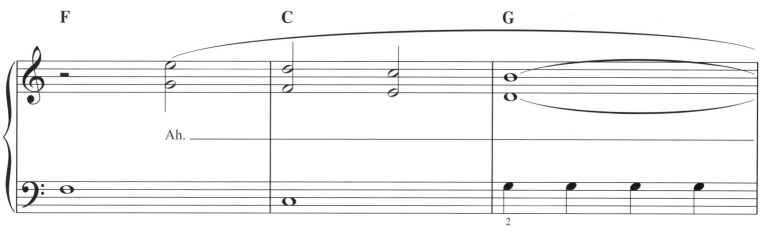

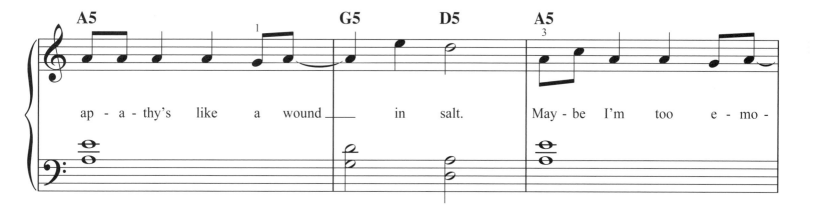

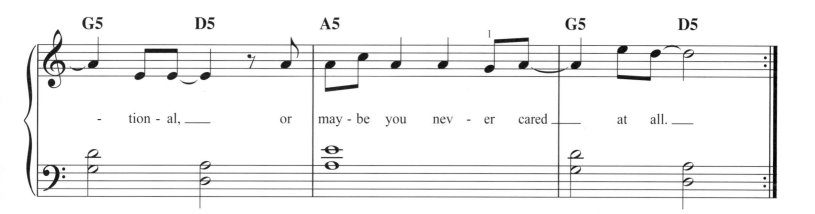

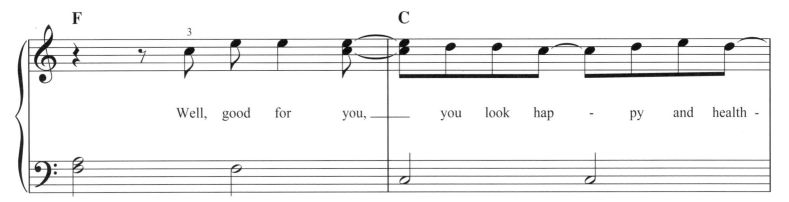

Well, good for you, ___ you look hap - py and health -

- y. Not me, if you ev - er cared _ to ask. ___ Good for you, _

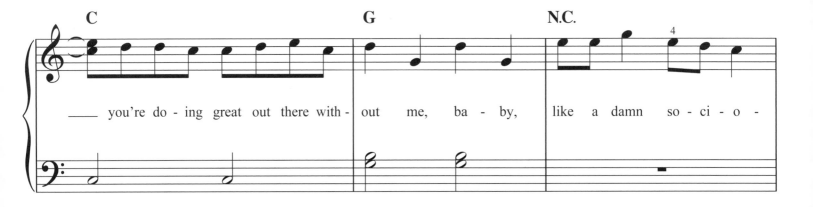

___ you're do - ing great out there with - out me, ba - by, like a damn so - ci - o -

path. I've lost my mind, _ I've spent the night ___ cry - ing on the

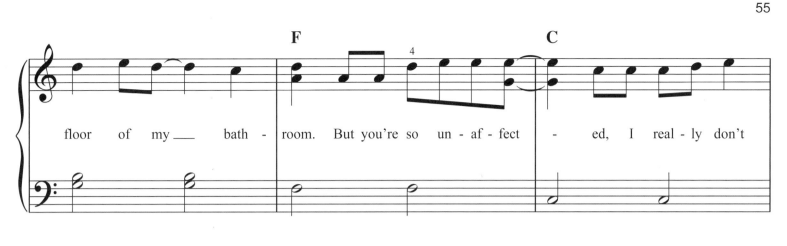

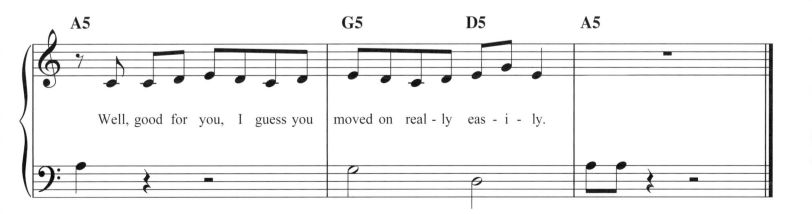

HOLD ON

Words and Music by JUSTIN BIEBER,
JON BELLION, ANDREW WATT,
WALTER DE BACKER, ALI TAMPOSI,
LUIZ BONFA and LOUIS BELL

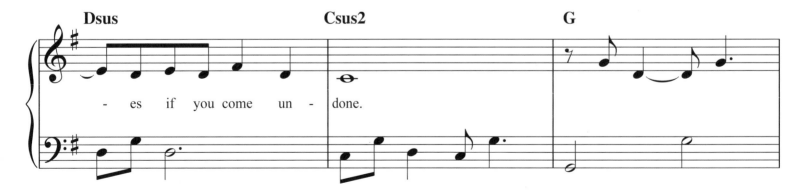

Painting stars upon your ceiling 'cause you wish that you could

find some feeling. Yeah, you, you know you can call ___ me if you need some -

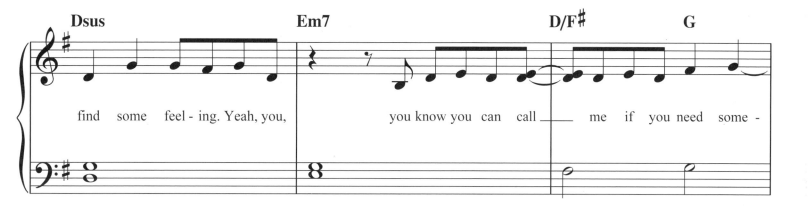

- one. ___ I need you to hold ___ on. Heaven is a place not too

far away. ___ We all know I should be the one to

say we all make mis - takes. __

Take my hand and

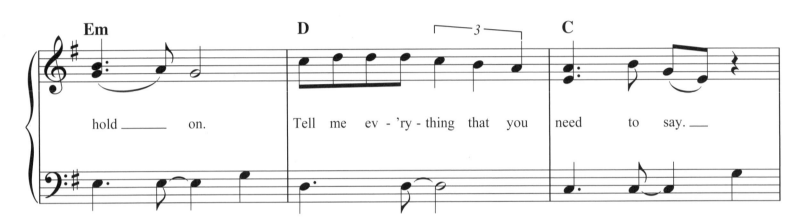

hold _____ on.

Tell me ev - 'ry - thing that you need to say. __

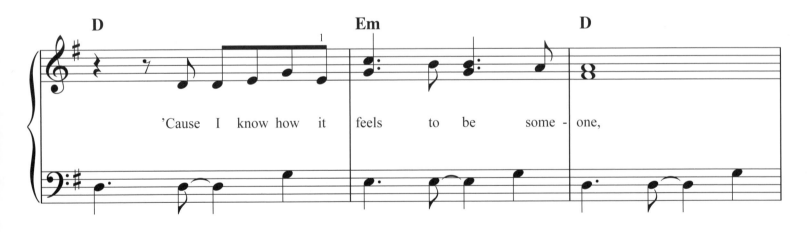

'Cause I know how it feels to be some - one,

feels to be some - one who los - es their way. __

Look - ing for an -

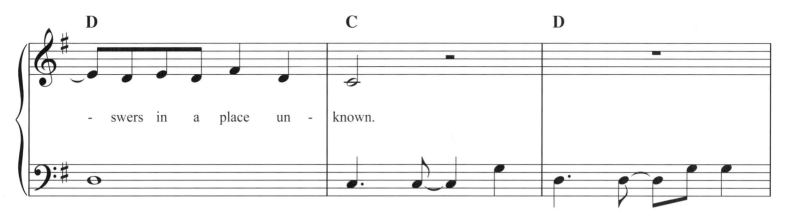

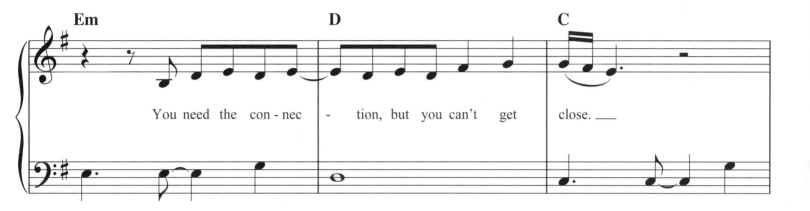

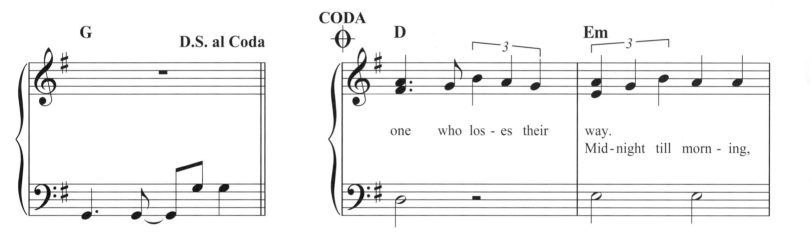

Mid - night till morn - ing, call if you need some-bod - y. I will be there for you.

I need you to hold _____ on. Heav-en is a place not too far a - way. _

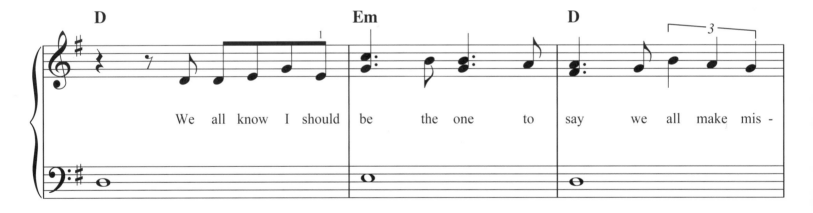

We all know I should be the one to say we all make mis -

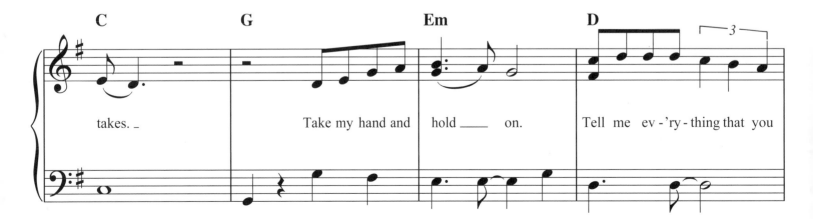

takes. _ Take my hand and hold _____ on. Tell me ev -'ry-thing that you

need to say. —   'Cause I know how it   feels   to be some - one,

feels   to be some - one   who los - es their   way.
Mid - night till morn - ing,

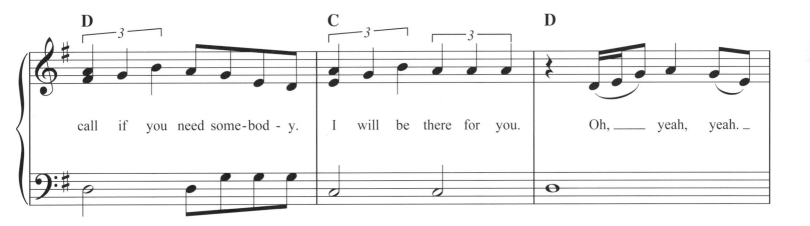

call   if you need some-bod - y.   I will be there for you.   Oh, ____ yeah,   yeah. __

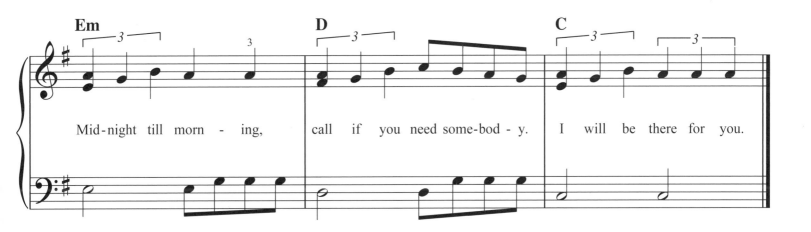

Mid-night till morn - ing,   call if you need some-bod - y.   I will be there for you.

HOLD ON TO ME

Words and Music by LAUREN DAIGLE,
PAUL DUNCAN and PAUL MABURY

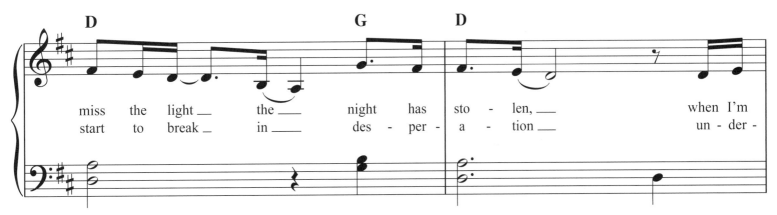

miss the light ____ the ____ night has sto - len, ____ when I'm
start to break ____ in ____ des - per - a - tion ____ un - der -

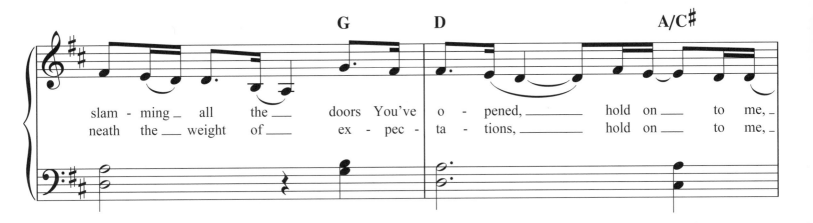

slam - ming ____ all the ____ doors You've o - pened, ____ hold on ____ to me, ____
neath the ____ weight of ____ ex - pec - ta - tions, ____ hold on ____ to me, ____

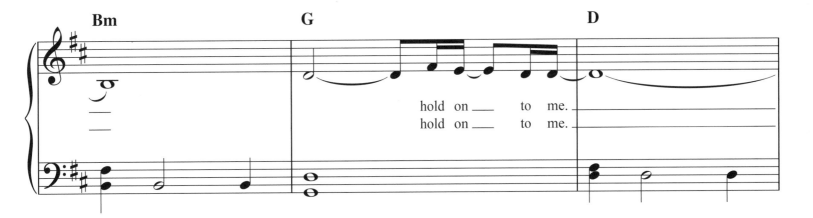

hold on ____ to me. ____
hold on ____ to me. ____

Hold on to me ____ when it's too dark to see ____

You, _____ when I _____ am sure _____ I have reached the end. _____

_____ Hold on to me _____ when I for - get _____ I need _____

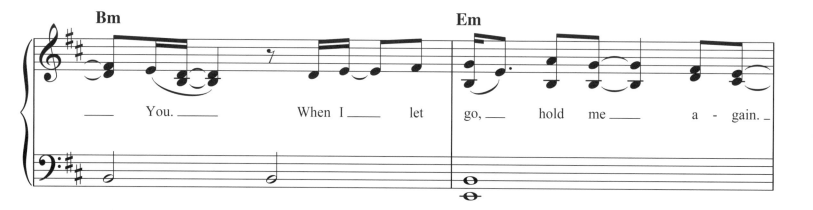

_____ You. _____ When I _____ let go, _____ hold me _____ a - gain. _____

When I _____

I could rest here ___ in Your ___ arms for -

ev - er _____ 'cause I know no - bod - y ___ loves me

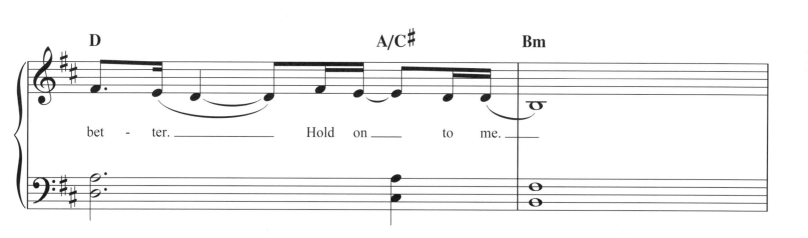

bet - ter. _____ Hold on ___ to me. ___

Hold on ___ to me. ___

LEAD THE WAY
from RAYA AND THE LAST DRAGON

Music and Lyrics by
JHENÉ AIKO

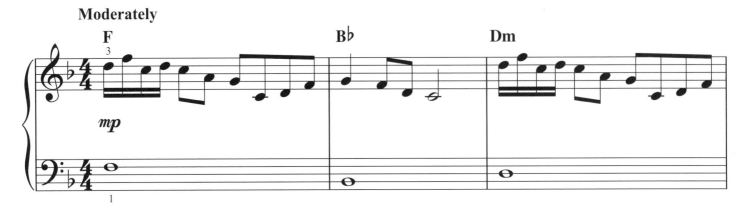

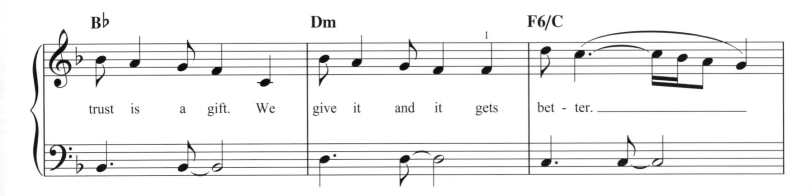

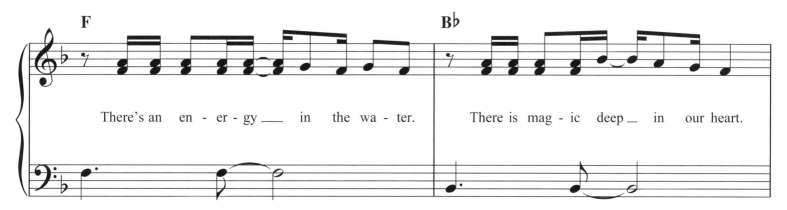

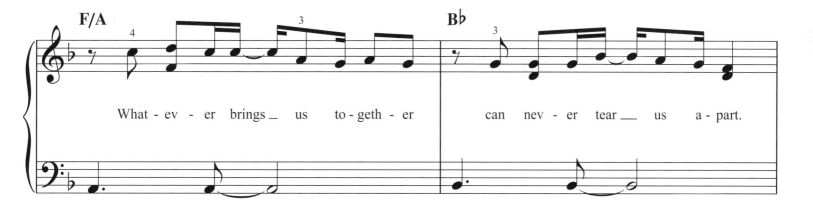

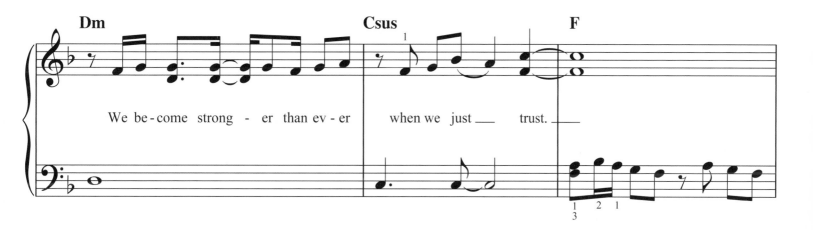

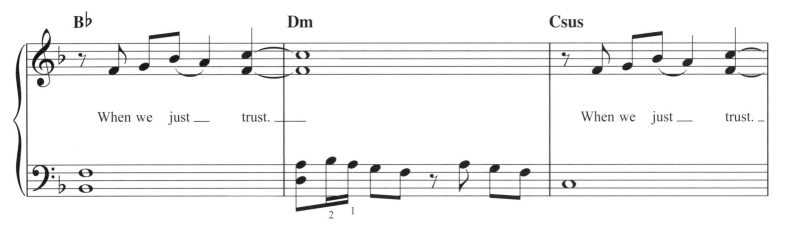

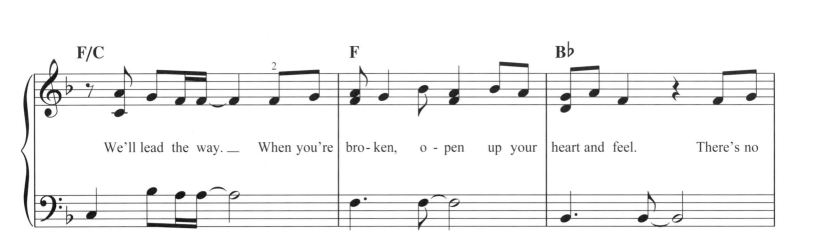

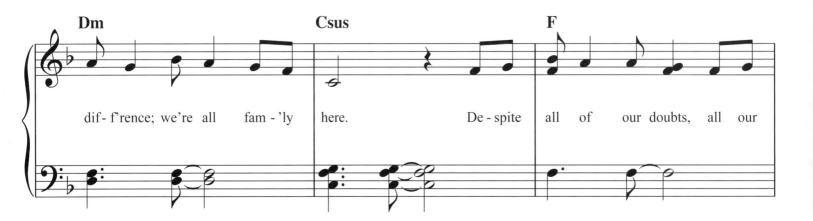

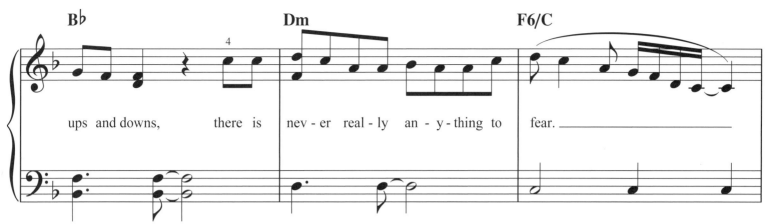

ups and downs, there is nev - er real - ly an - y - thing to fear. ____

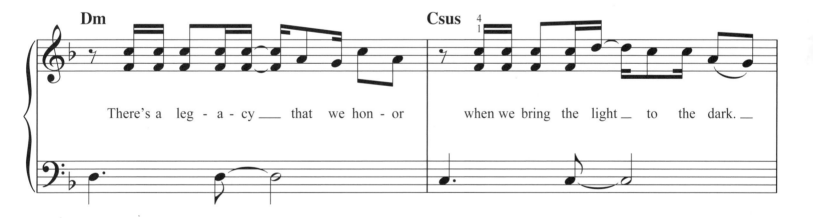

There's an en - er - gy ___ in the wa - ter. There is mag - ic deep _ in our heart.

There's a leg - a - cy ___ that we hon - or when we bring the light _ to the dark. _

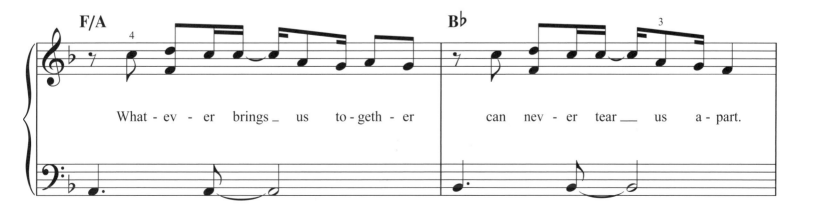

What - ev - er brings _ us to - geth - er can nev - er tear ___ us a - part.

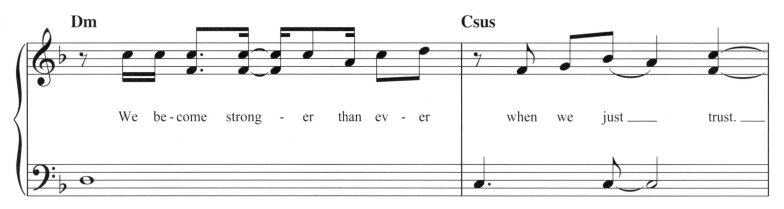

We be-come strong - er than ev - er   when we just ___ trust. ___

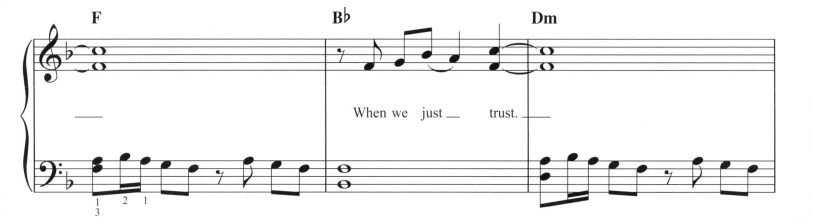

___   When we just ___ trust. ___

When we just ___ trust. ___   When we just ___ trust. _

___   We'll lead the way. ___

To Coda

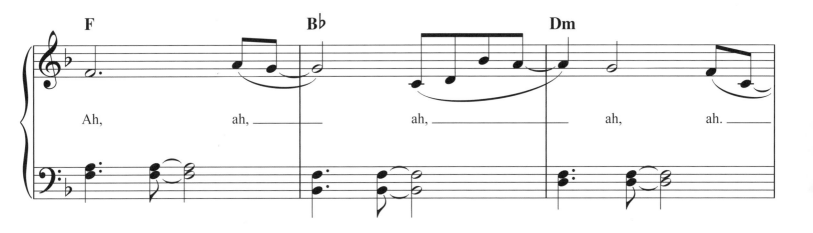

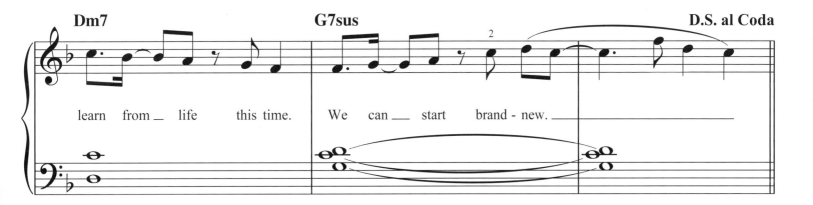

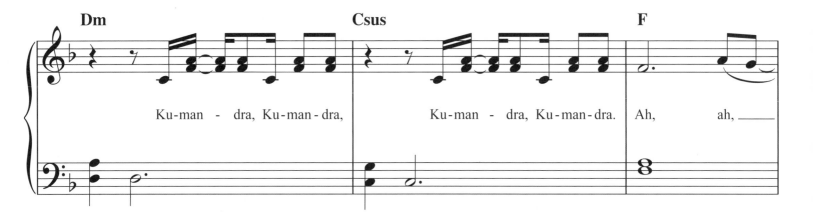

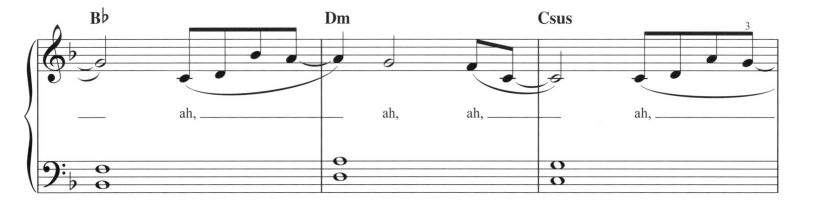

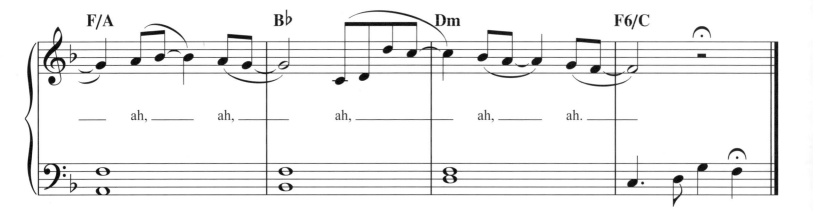

LEAVE THE DOOR OPEN

Words and Music by BRUNO MARS,
DERNST EMILE, CHRISTOPHER BRODY BROWN
and BRANDON PAAK ANDERSON

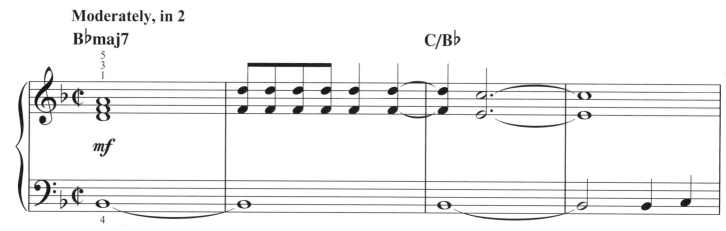

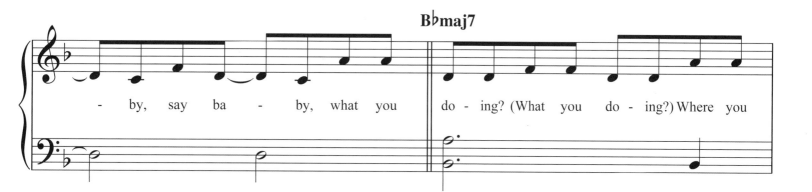

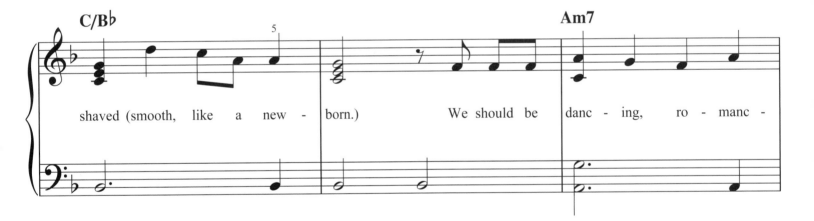

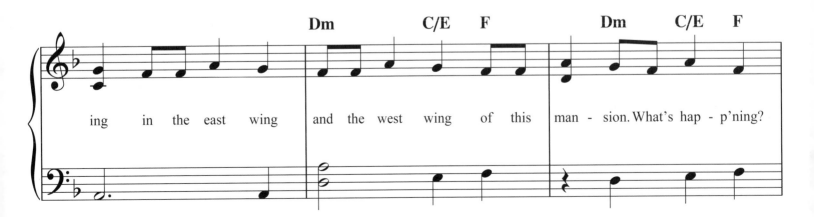

I ain't play-ing no games. Ev - 'ry word that I say

_____ is com-ing straight from the heart. So, if you're tryin' to

lay in these arms, _____ I'm - a leave the door o - pen.

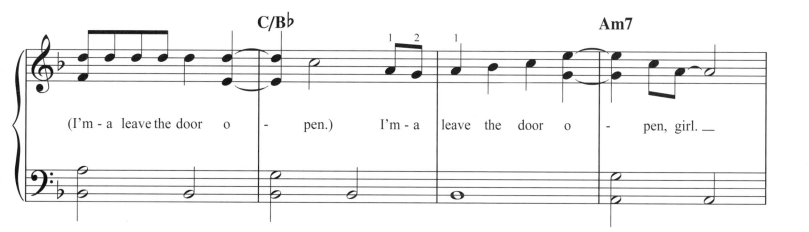

(I'm - a leave the door o - pen.) I'm - a leave the door o - pen, girl. __

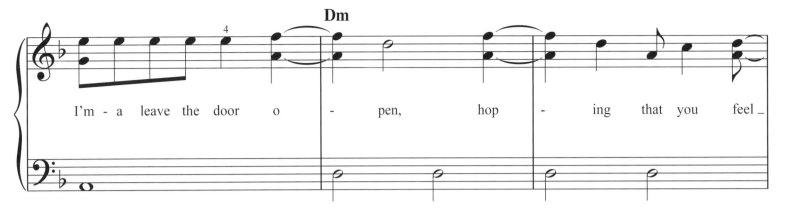

I'm-a leave the door o - pen, hop - ing that you feel

the way I feel and you want me like I want you to - night, ba - by.

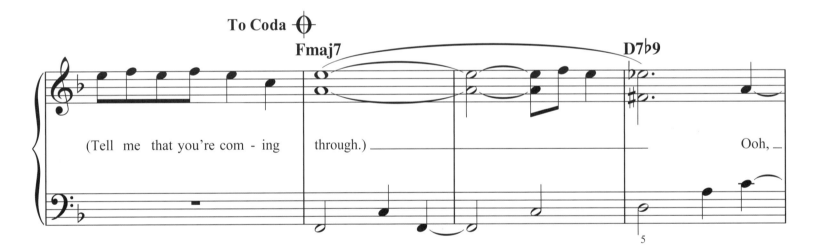

(Tell me that you're com - ing through.) Ooh,

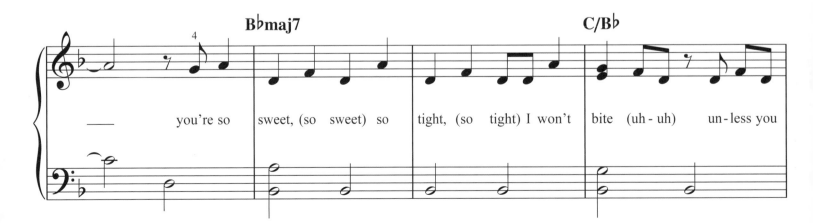

you're so sweet, (so sweet) so tight, (so tight) I won't bite (uh - uh) un-less you

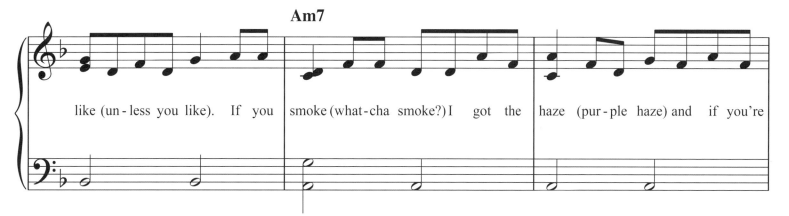

like (un-less you like). If you smoke (what-cha smoke?) I got the haze (pur-ple haze) and if you're

hun-gry, girl, I got fi - lets. Ooh, ba - by, don't keep me wait - ing. There's

so much love we could be mak - ing. (Sha - mone.) I'm talk - ing kiss - ing, cud -

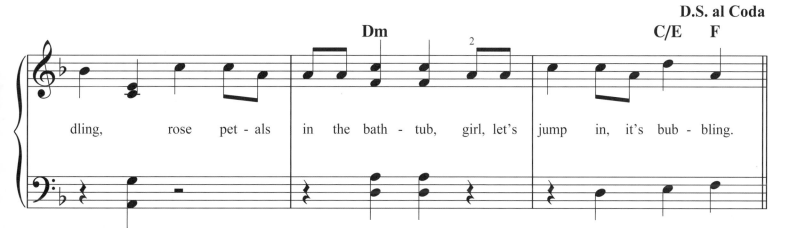

dling, rose pet - als in the bath - tub, girl, let's jump in, it's bub - bling.

through.)

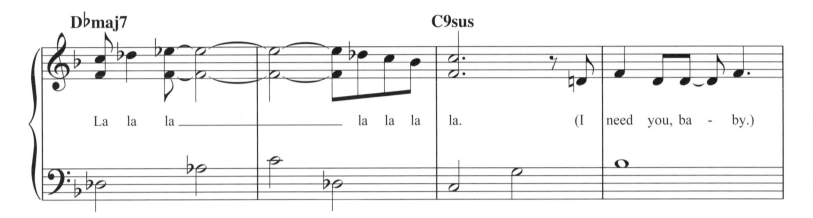

La la la _____ la la la la. (I need you, ba - by.)

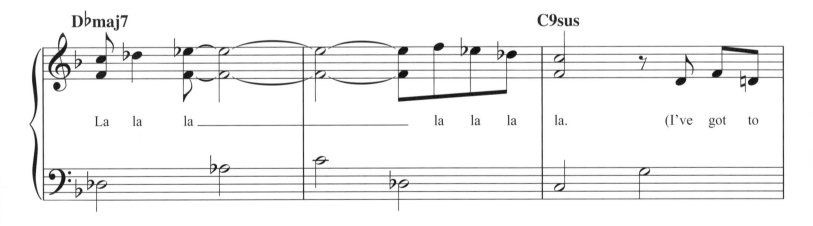

La la la _____ la la la la. (I've got to

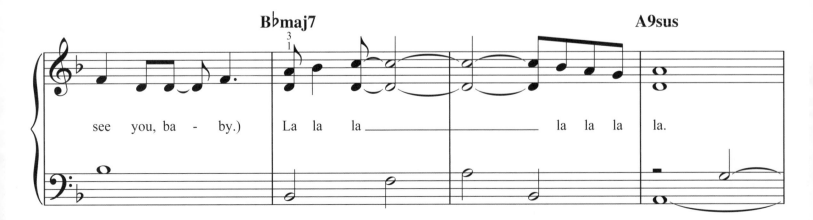

see you, ba - by.) La la la _____ la la la la.

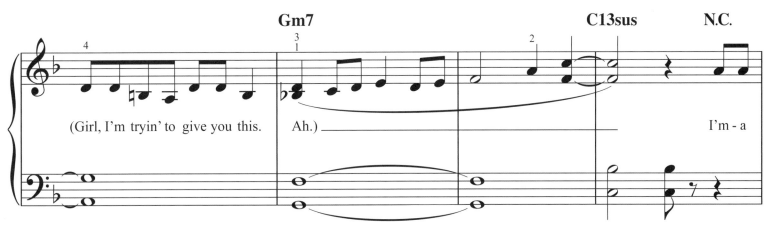

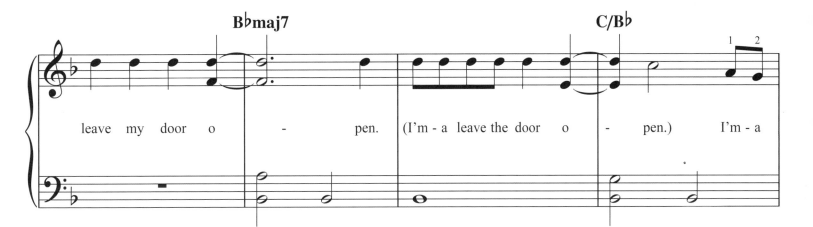

want me like I want you to - night, ___ ba - by. (Tell me that you're com - ing

through.) ___

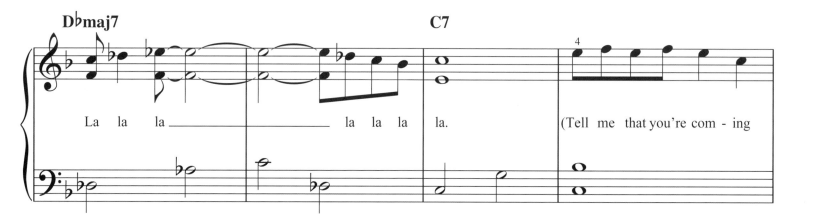

La la la ___ la la la la. (Tell me that you're com - ing

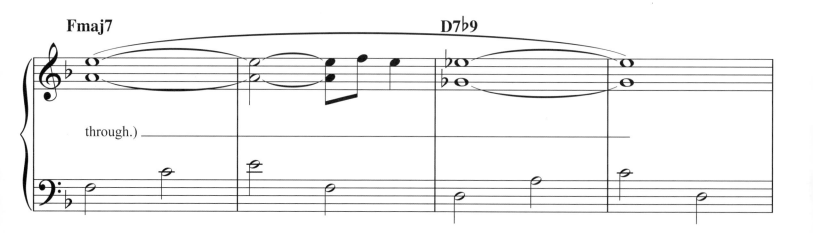

through.) ___

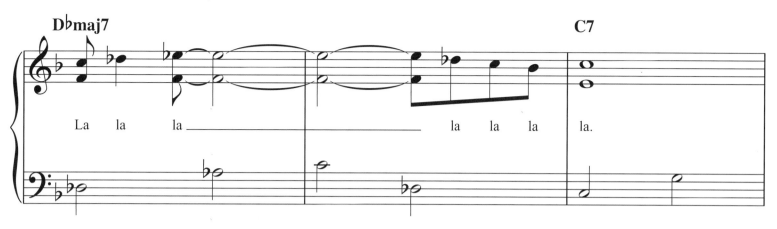

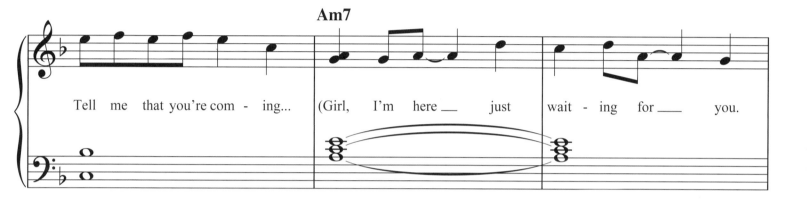

LEVITATING

Words and Music by DUA LIPA,
STEPHEN KOZMENIUK, CLARENCE COFFEE JR.
and SARAH HUDSON

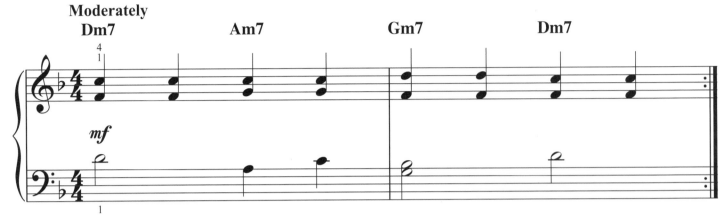

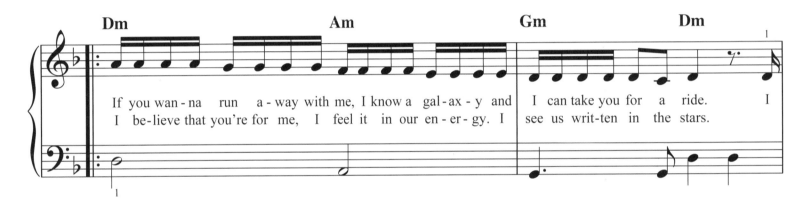

If you wan-na run a-way with me, I know a gal-ax-y and I can take you for a ride. I
I be-lieve that you're for me, I feel it in our en-er-gy. I see us writ-ten in the stars.

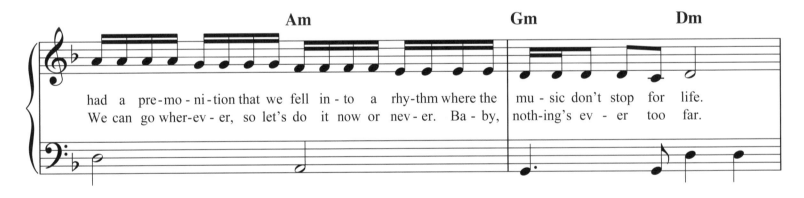

had a pre-mo-ni-tion that we fell in-to a rhy-thm where the mu-sic don't stop for life.
We can go wher-ev-er, so let's do it now or nev-er. Ba-by, noth-ing's ev-er too far.

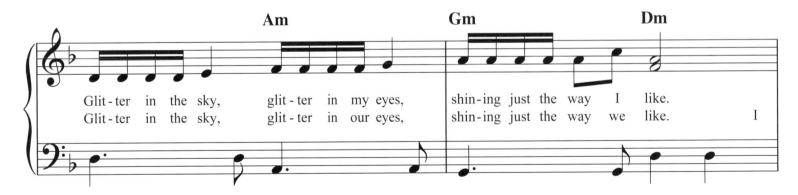

Glit-ter in the sky, glit-ter in my eyes, shin-ing just the way I like.
Glit-ter in the sky, glit-ter in our eyes, shin-ing just the way we like. I

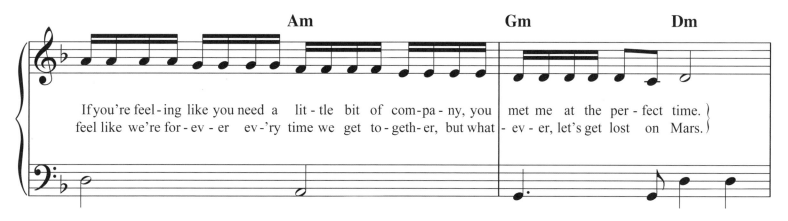

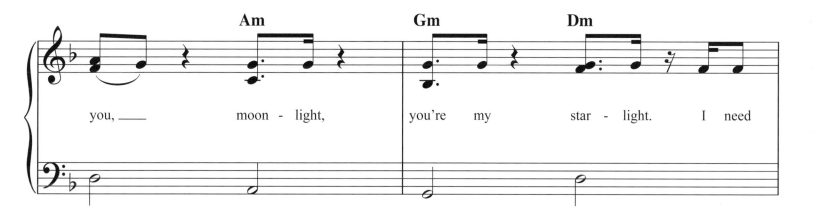

you ___ all night. Come on, dance _ with me. I'm lev - i - tat - ing.

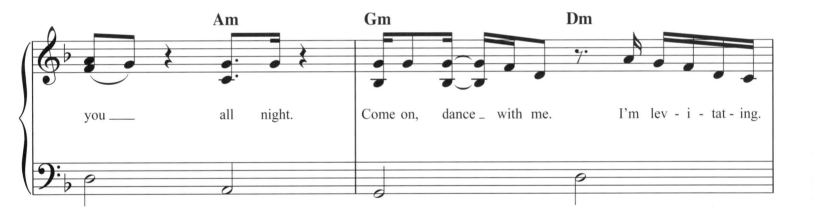

You, ___ moon - light, you're my star - light. I need

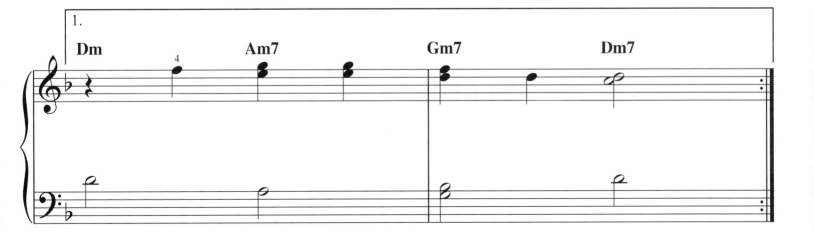

you ___ all night. Come on, dance _ with me. I'm lev - i - tat - ing.

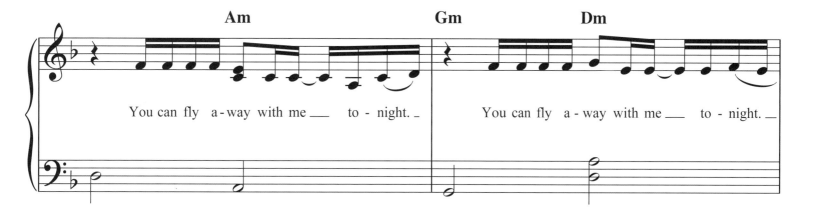

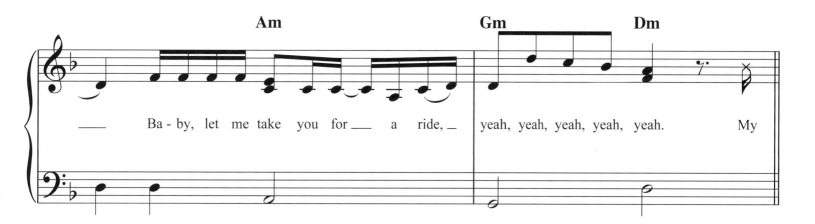

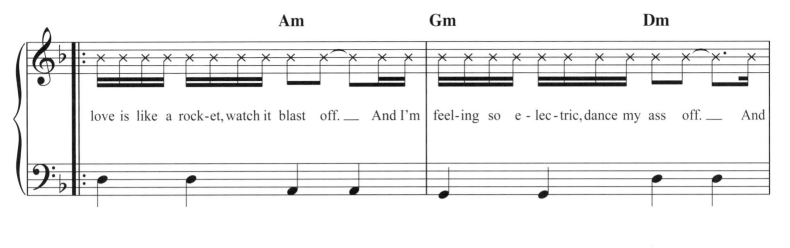

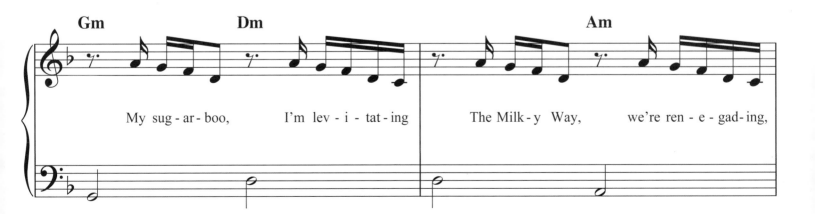

I got you, — moon-light, you're my star-light. I need

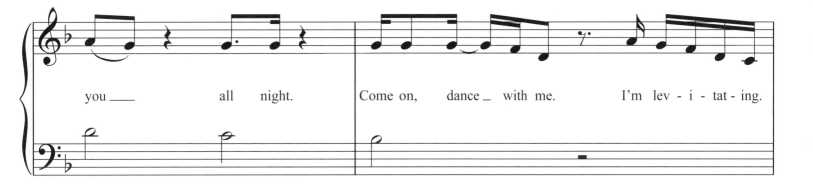

you — all night. Come on, dance — with me. I'm lev-i-tat-ing.

You can fly a-way with me — to-night. — You can fly a-way with me — to-night. —

— Ba-by, let me take you for — a ride, — yeah, yeah, yeah, yeah, yeah. I'm lev-i-tat-ing.

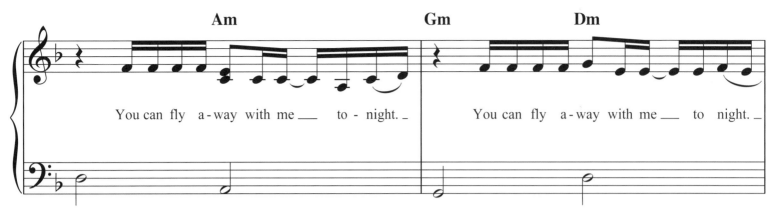

You can fly a-way with me ___ to - night. ___ You can fly a-way with me ___ to night. ___

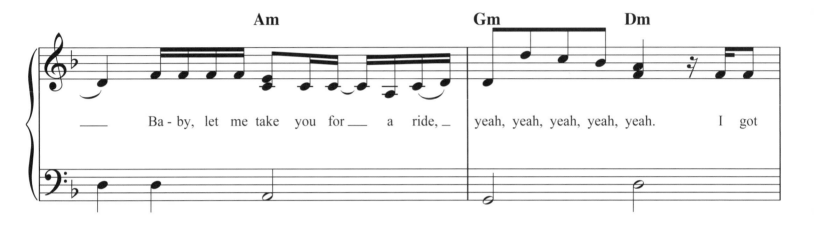

___ Ba - by, let me take you for ___ a ride, ___ yeah, yeah, yeah, yeah, yeah. I got

you, ___ moon - light, you're my star - light. I need

you ___ all night. Come on, dance ___ with me. I'm lev - i - tat - ing.

LOST CAUSE

Words and Music by BILLIE EILISH O'CONNELL
and FINNEAS O'CONNELL

Moderately slow

Some-thing's in the...

Some-thing's in the

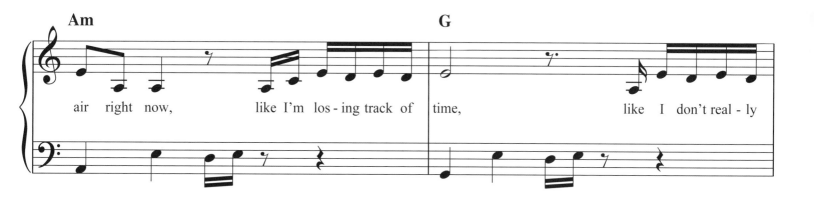

air right now, like I'm los-ing track of time, like I don't real-ly

care right now. But may-be that's fine. You weren't e - ven

there that day   I was wait-ing on ___ you.   I won-der if you were a-

ware that day   was the last   straw for me,   and I   know...

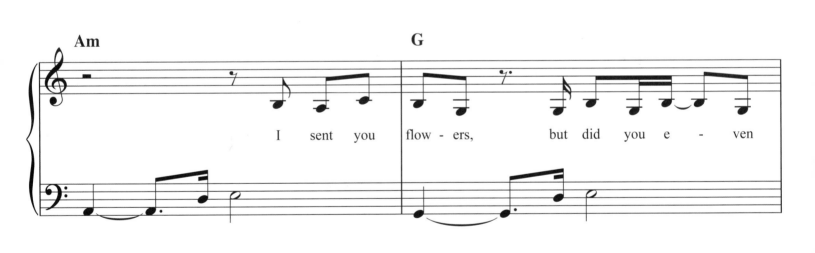

I sent you   flow - ers,   but did you e - ven

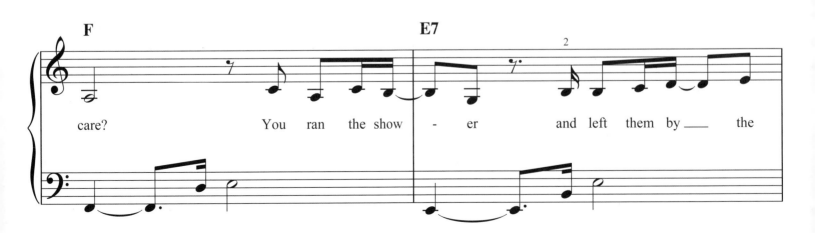

care?   You ran the show - er   and left them by ___ the

stairs. _____   Thought you

had your stuff to-geth-er, but damn, I was wrong. ___ You ain't noth-ing but a lost cause, _

___ and this ain't noth-ing like it once was. ___ I know you think you're such an out - law, _

___ but you got no job. ___ You ain't noth-ing but a lost cause, _

4

and this ain't noth-ing like it once was. ___ I know you think you're such an out - law, ___

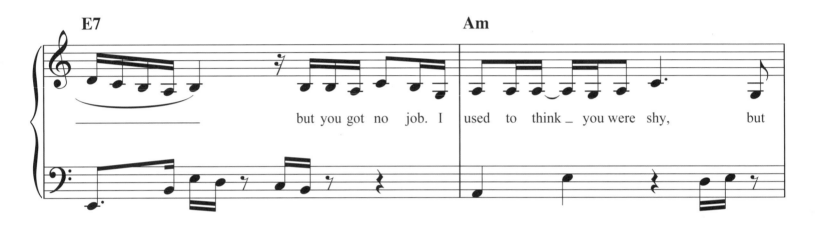

but you got no job. I used to think ___ you were shy, but

may - be you ___ just had noth-ing on your mind. May - be you ___ were think - ing 'bout ___ your -

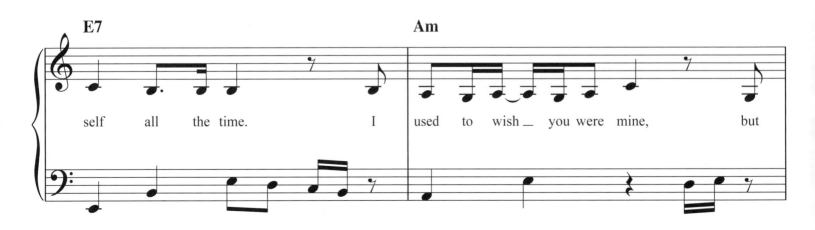

self all the time. I used to wish ___ you were mine, but

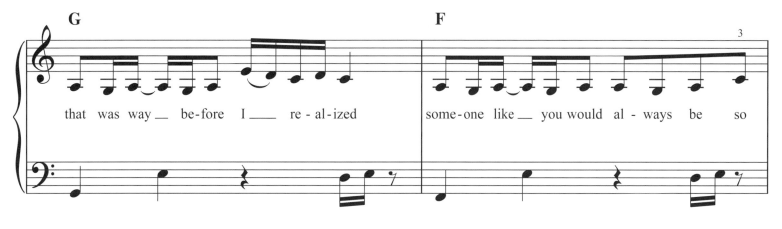

that was way — be-fore I —— re - al-ized

some-one like — you would al - ways be so

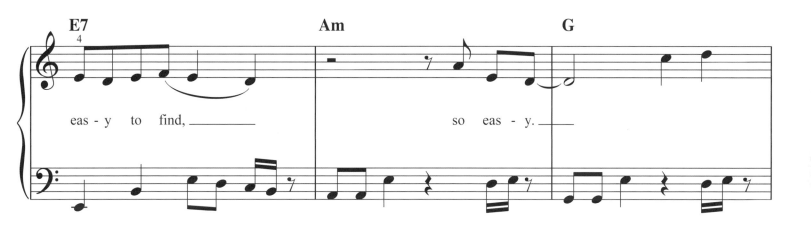

eas - y to find, ————

so eas - y. ——

Gave me no

flow - ers. Wish I did - n't care.

You'd been gone for

You ain't noth-ing but a lost cause, and this ain't noth-ing like it once was.

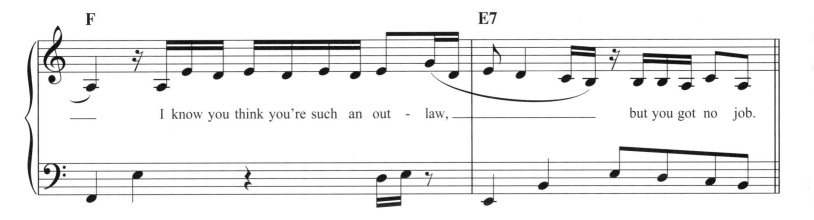

I know you think you're such an out - law, but you got no job.

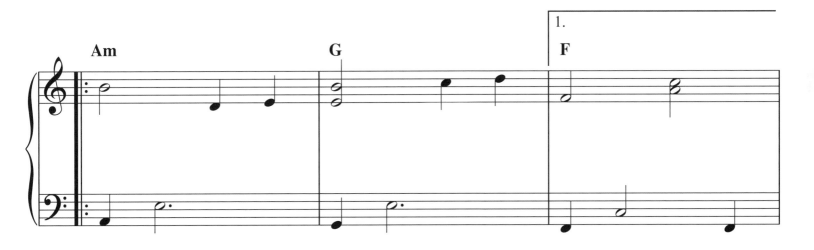

1.

2.

SAVE YOUR TEARS

Words and Music by ABEL TESFAYE,
MAX MARTIN, JASON QUENNEVILLE,
OSCAR HOLTER and AHMAD BALSHE

Moderate Pop

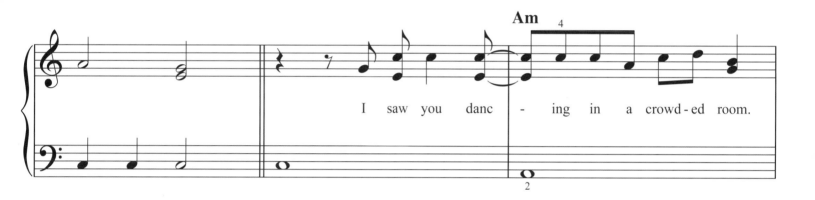

I saw you danc - ing in a crowd-ed room.

You look so hap - py when I'm not with you. But then you saw

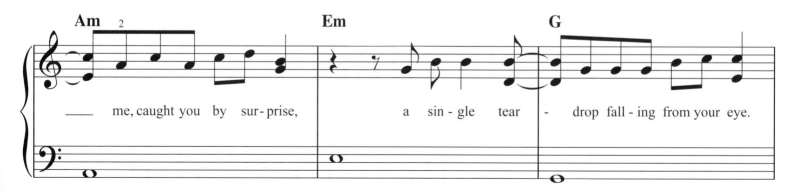

me, caught you by sur - prise, a sin - gle tear - drop fall-ing from your eye.

I don't know why   I   run a - way.

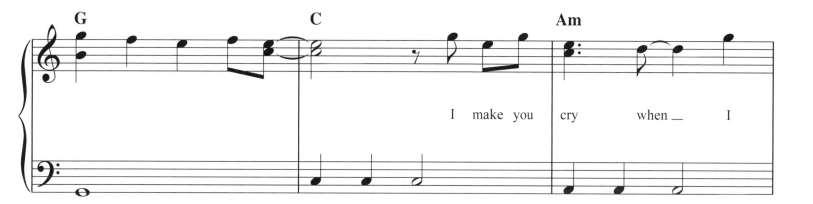

I make you   cry   when __   I

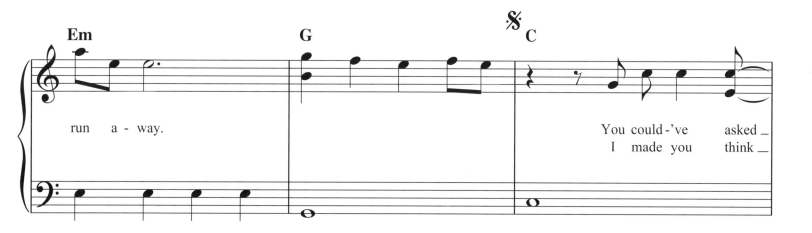

run a - way.

You could -'ve   asked __
I made you   think __

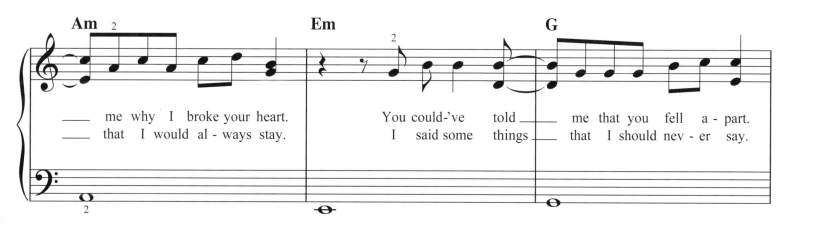

__ me why I broke your heart.
__ that I would al - ways stay.

You could -'ve   told ____ __ me that you   fell a - part.
I said some   things ____ __ that I should nev - er say.

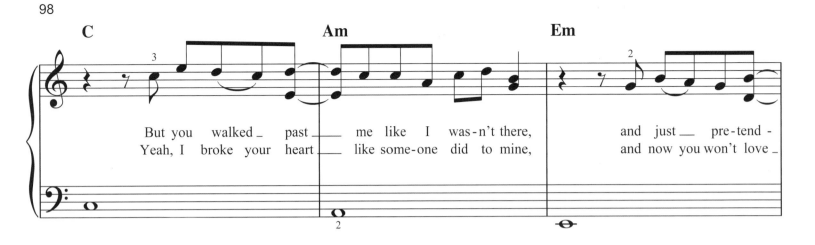

But you walked — past — me like I was-n't there,
Yeah, I broke your heart — like some-one did to mine,

and just — pre-tend -
and now you won't love —

- ed like you did-n't care. —
— me for a sec-ond time. —

I don't know why I

run a-way.

I make you

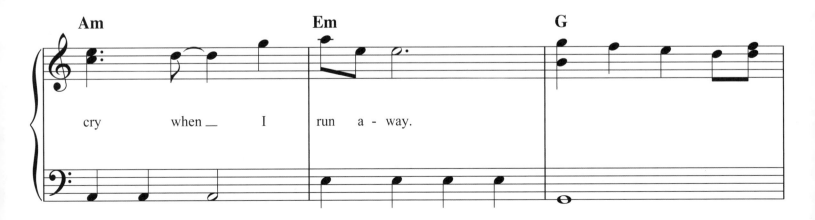

cry when — I run a-way.

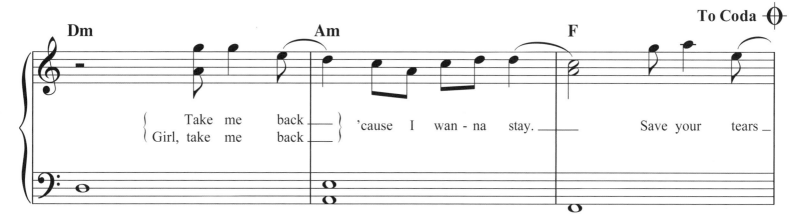

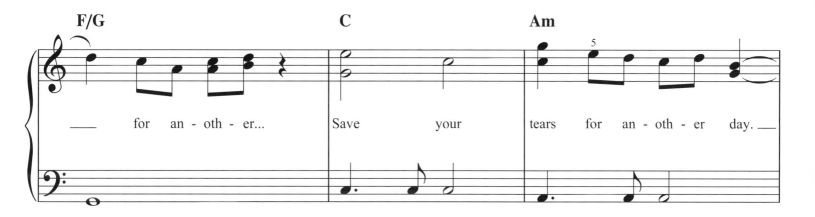

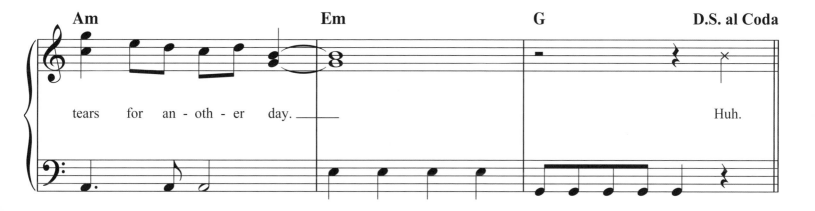

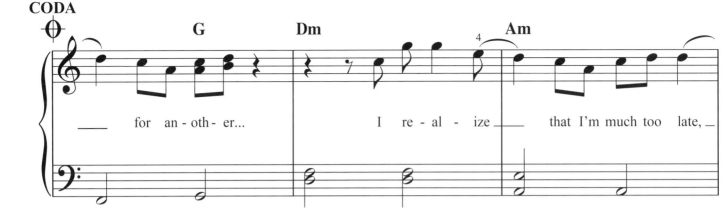

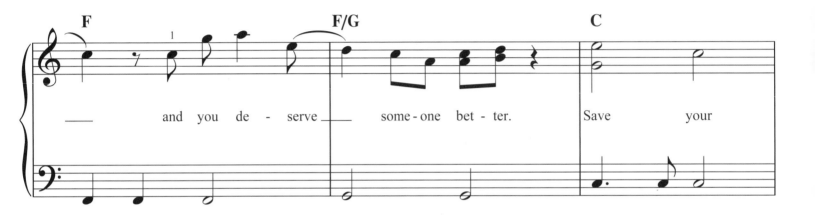

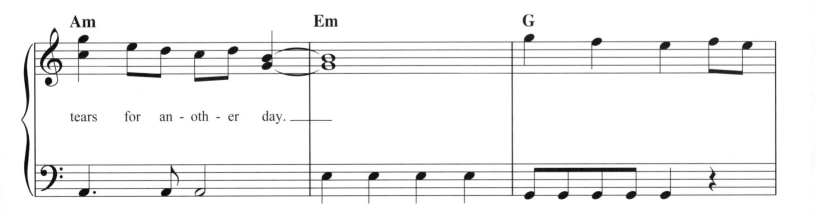

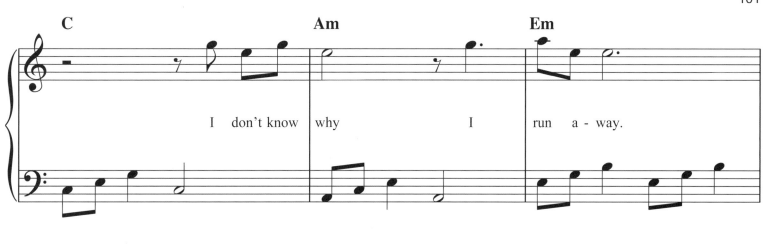

I don't know why I run a - way.

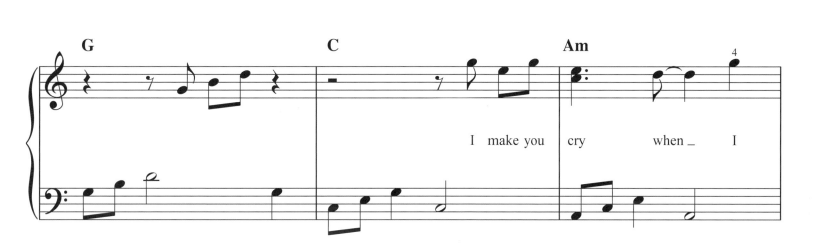

I make you cry when _ I

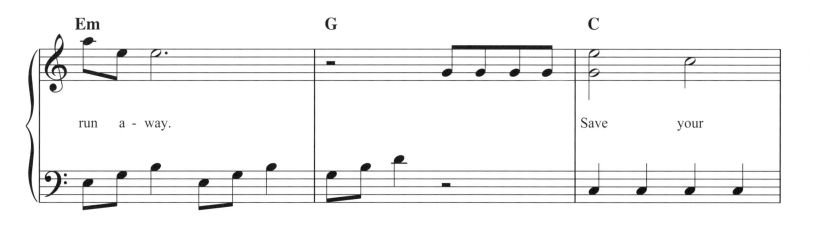

run a - way. Save your

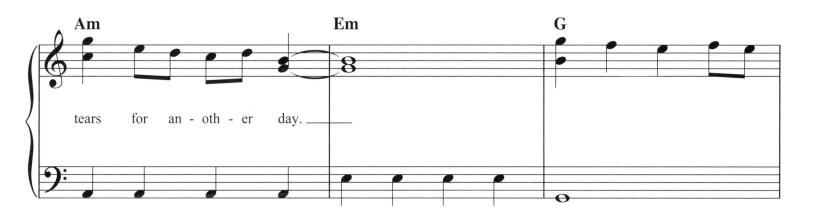

tears for an - oth - er day. _

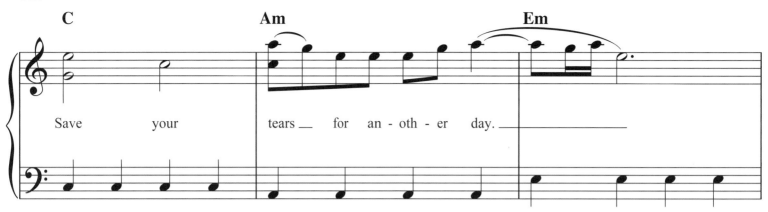

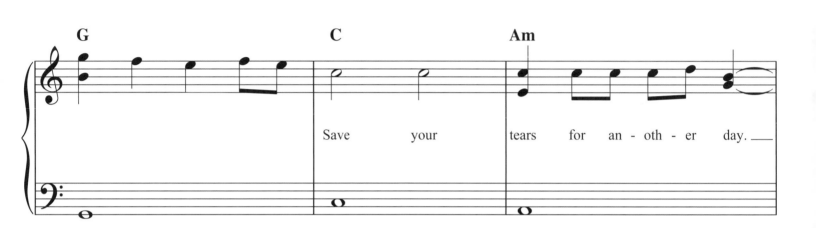

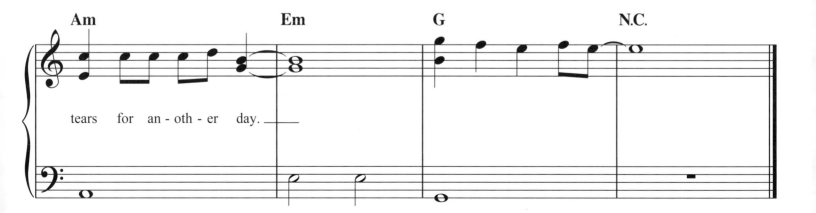

SOLAR POWER

Words and Music by ELLA YELICH-O'CONNOR
and JACK ANTONOFF

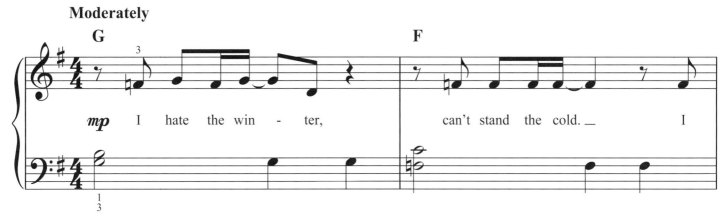

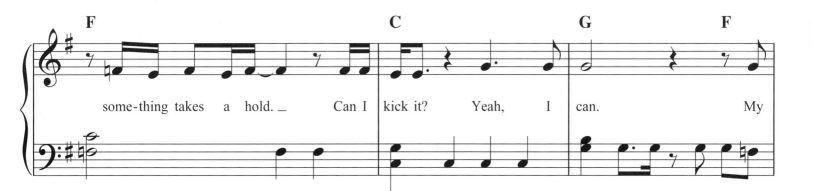

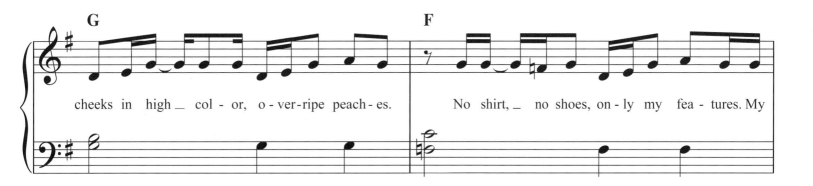

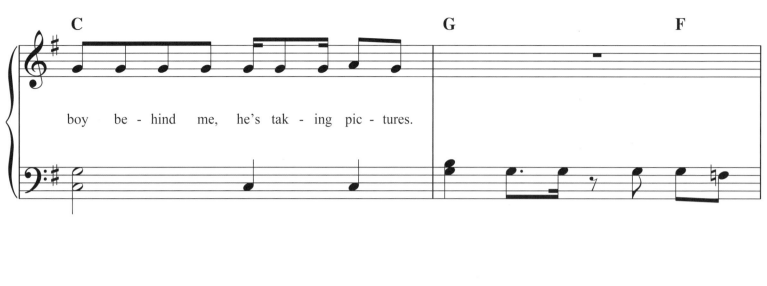

boy be - hind me, he's tak - ing pic - tures.

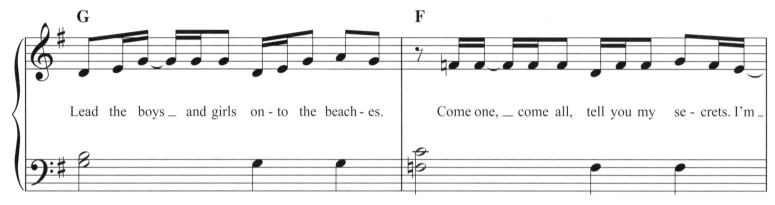

Lead the boys _ and girls on - to the beach - es. Come one, _ come all, tell you my se - crets. I'm _

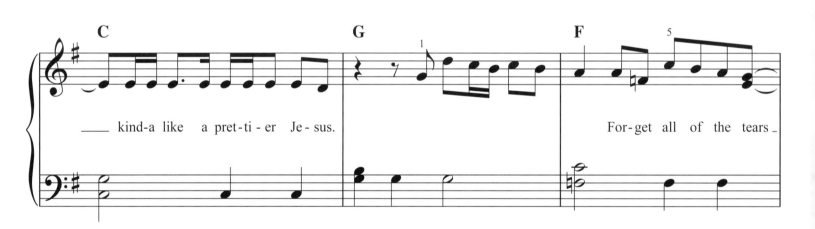

_ kind-a like a pret-ti-er Je - sus. For-get all of the tears _

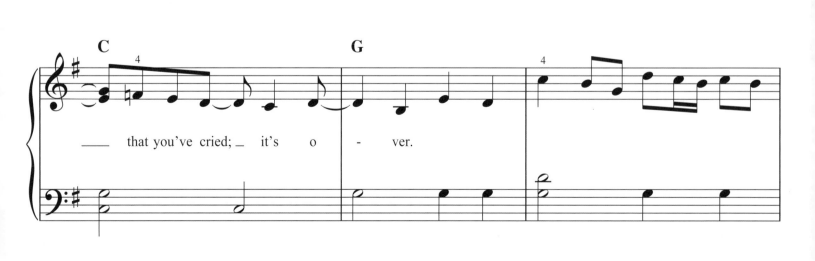

_ that you've cried; _ it's o - ver.

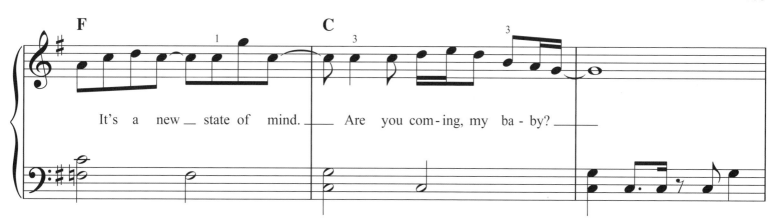

cheeks in high __ col - or, o - ver-ripe peach - es.   No shirt, __ no shoes, on - ly my fea - tures. My

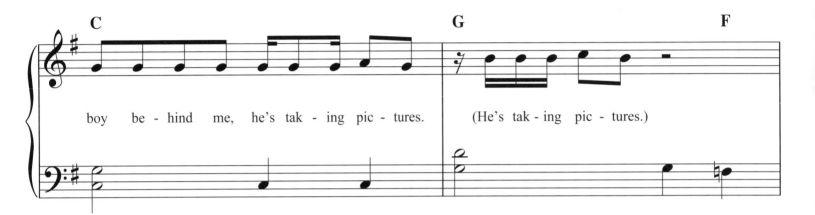

boy be - hind me, he's tak - ing pic - tures.   (He's tak - ing pic - tures.)

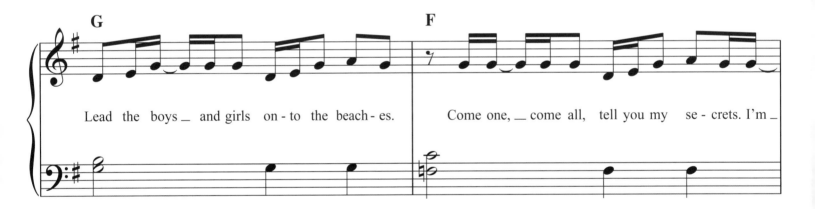

Lead the boys __ and girls on - to the beach- es.   Come one, __ come all, tell you my se - crets. I'm __

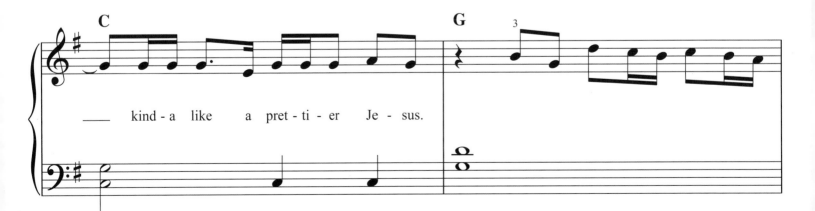

__ kind - a like a pret - ti - er Je - sus.

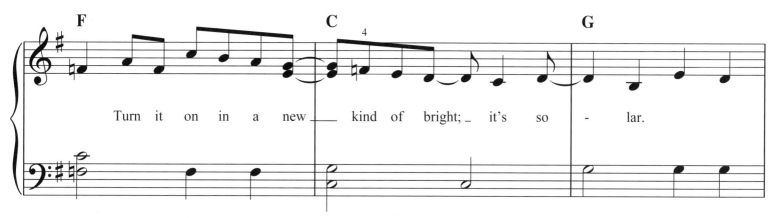

Turn it on in a new __ kind of bright; _ it's so - lar.

Come on and let the bliss be - gin. __

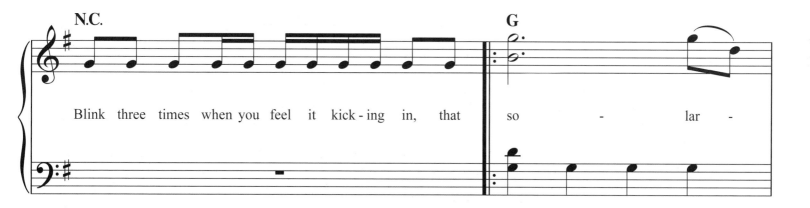

Blink three times when you feel it kick - ing in, that so - lar -

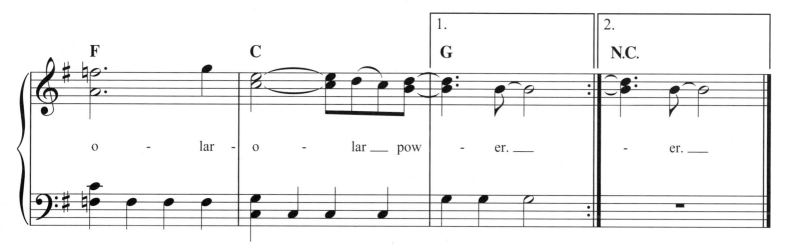

o - lar - o - lar __ pow - er. __ - er. __

SHY AWAY

Words and Music by
TYLER JOSEPH

Bright Rock, in 2

When I get _____

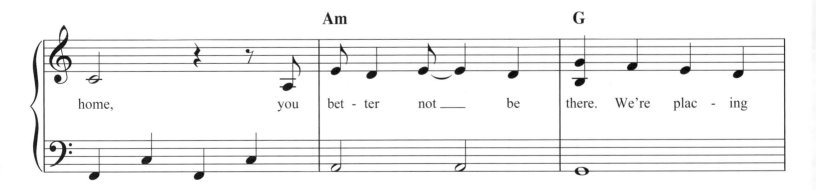

home, you bet - ter not _____ be there. We're plac - ing

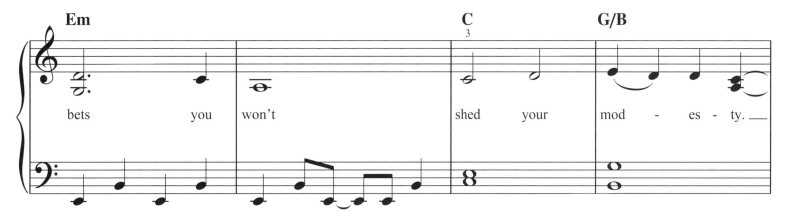

Em bets you won't | shed your | **C** **G/B** mod - es - ty. ___

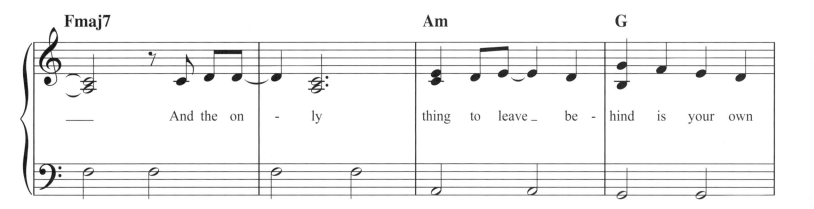

Fmaj7 ___ And the on - ly | thing to leave ___ be - **Am** hind is your own **G**

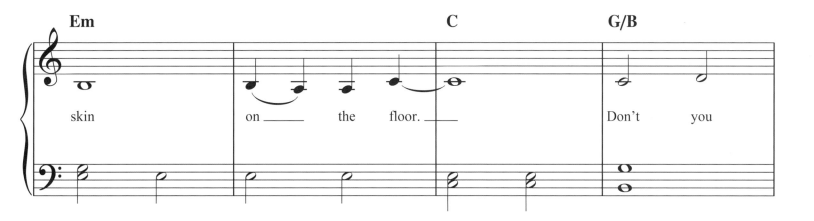

Em skin | on ___ the floor. ___ | **C** **G/B** Don't you

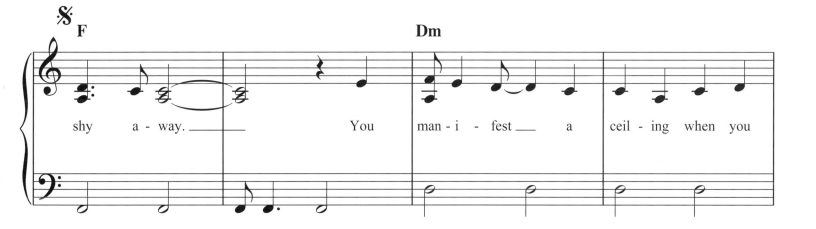

F shy a - way. ___ You | man - i - fest ___ a **Dm** ceil - ing when you

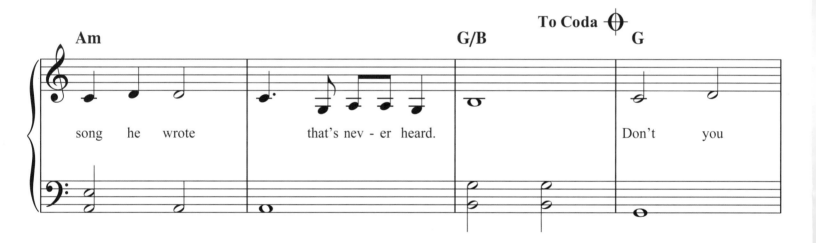

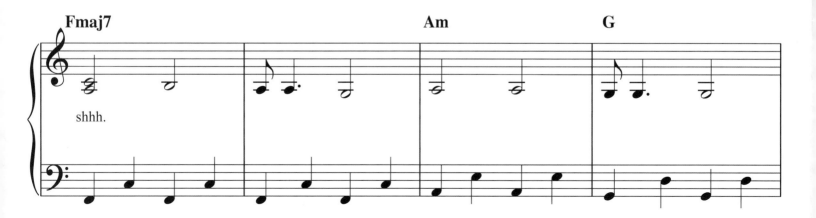

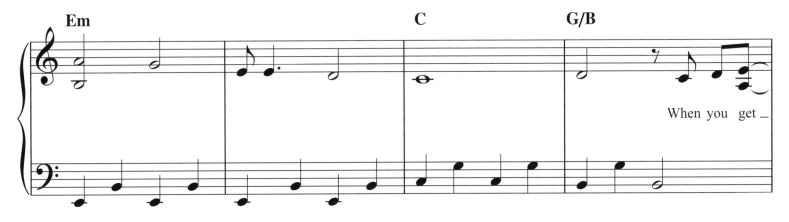

When you get _

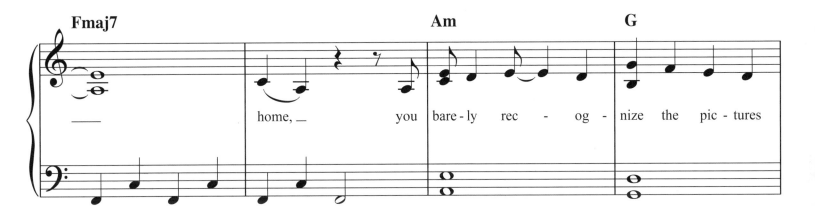

_ home, _ you bare-ly rec - og - nize the pic - tures

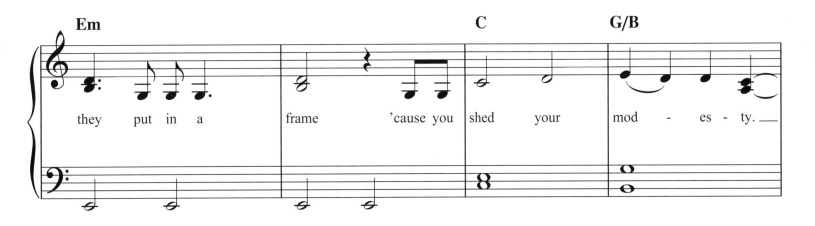

they put in a frame 'cause you shed your mod - es - ty. _

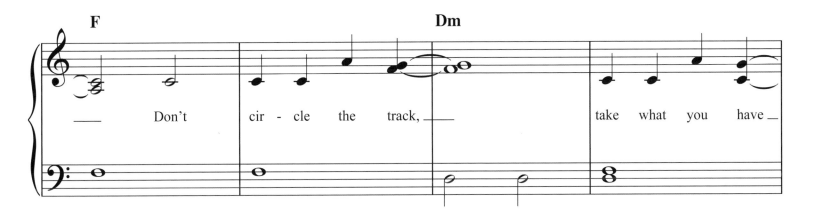

_ Don't cir - cle the track, _ take what you have _

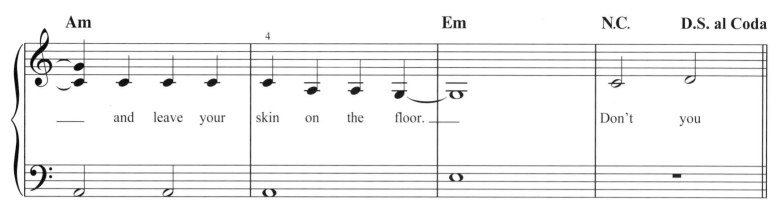

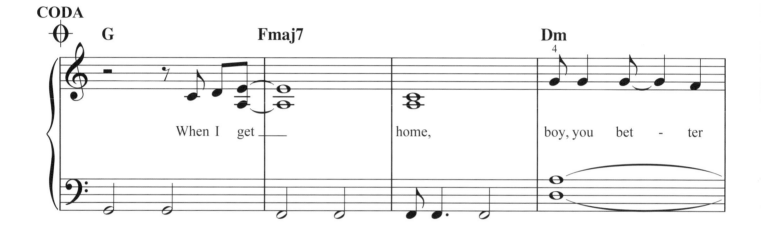

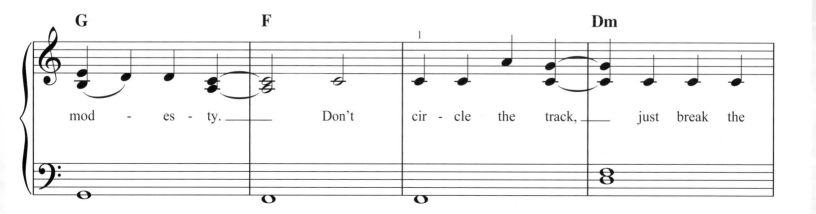

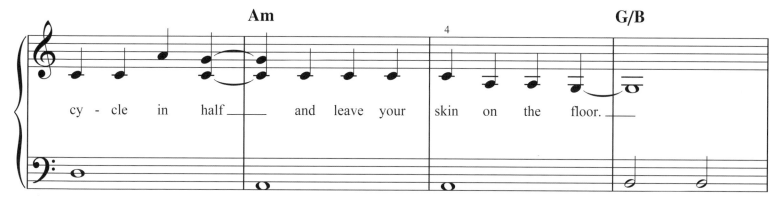

cy - cle   in   half____   and   leave   your   skin   on   the   floor.____

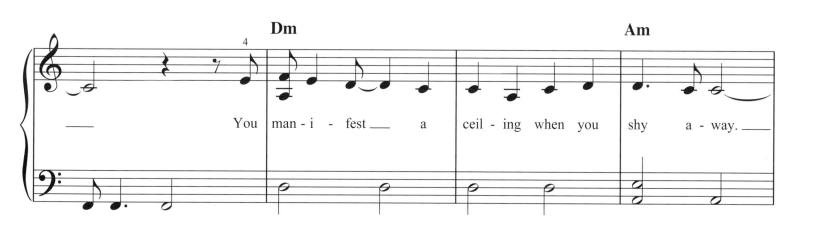

Don't   you   shy   a - way.____

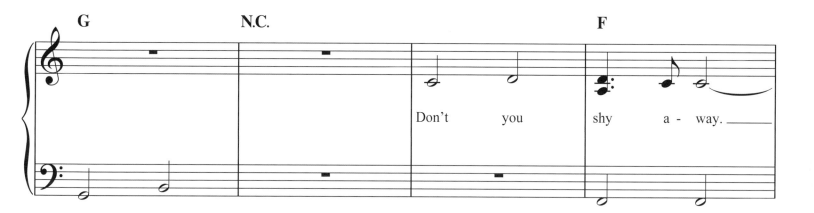

____   You   man - i - fest____   a   ceil - ing   when   you   shy   a - way.____

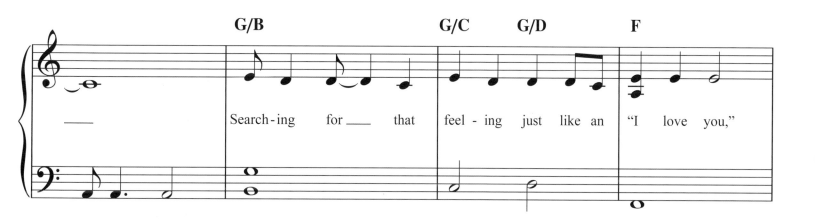

____   Search - ing   for ____   that   feel - ing   just   like   an   "I   love   you,"

(ooh, ooh, ooh) — that is - n't words, — (bah, bah, bah) — like a song he wrote

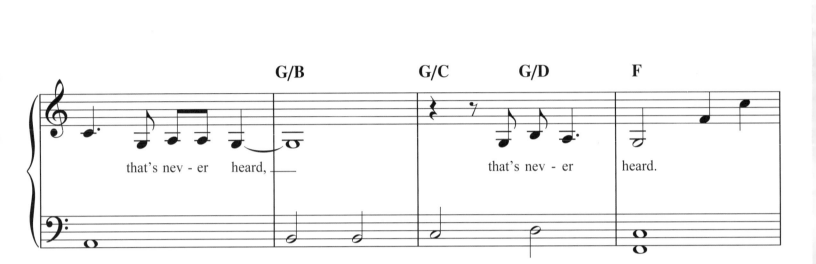

that's nev - er heard, — that's nev - er heard.

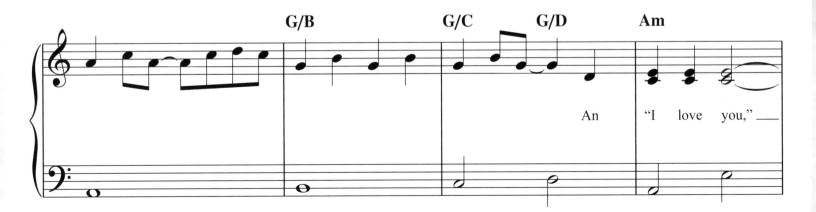

An "I love you," —

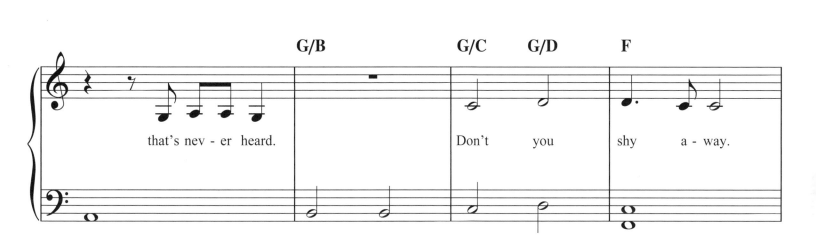

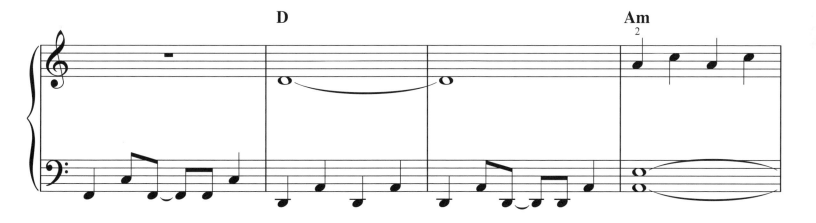

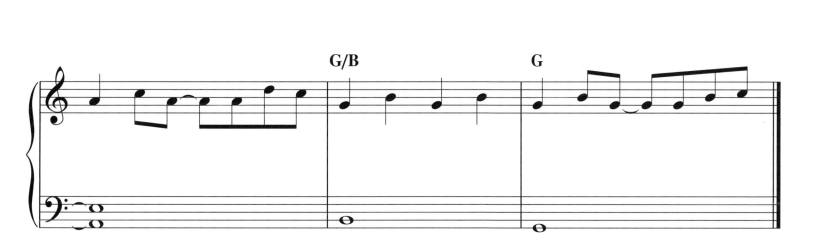

YOUR POWER

Words and Music by BILLIE EILISH O'CONNELL
and FINNEAS O'CONNELL

Moderately fast

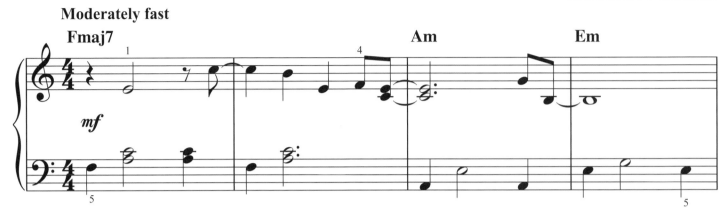

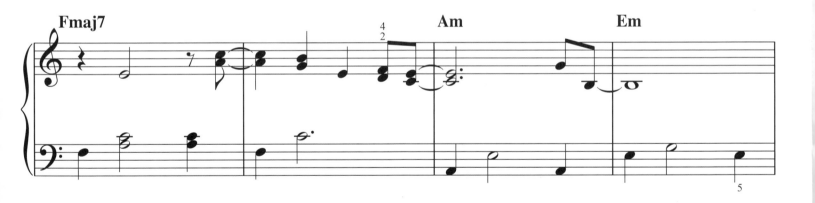

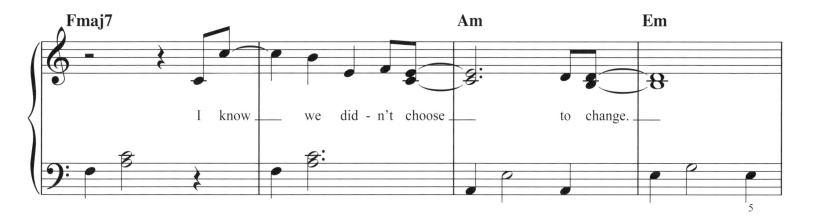

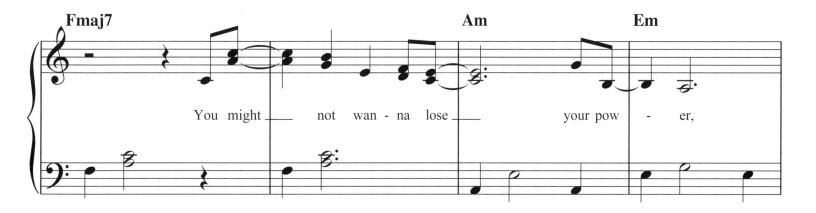

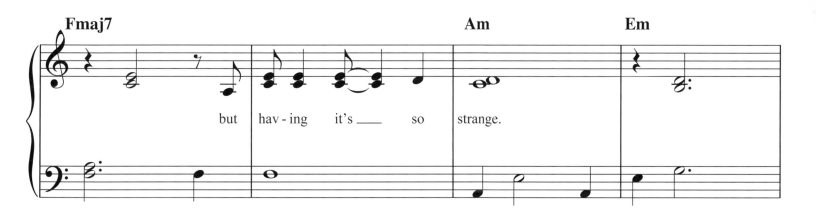

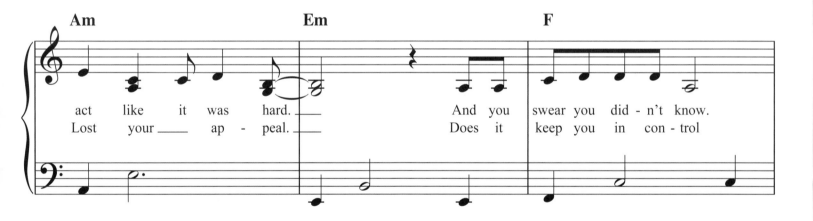

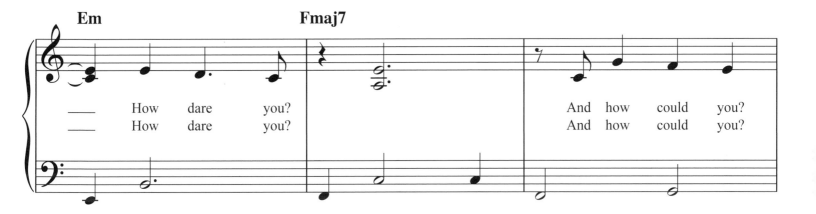

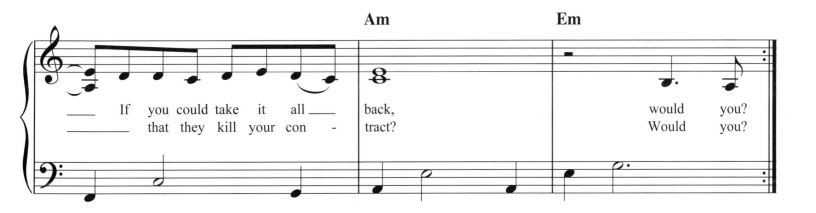

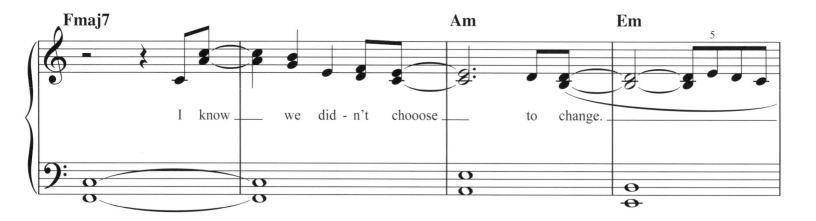

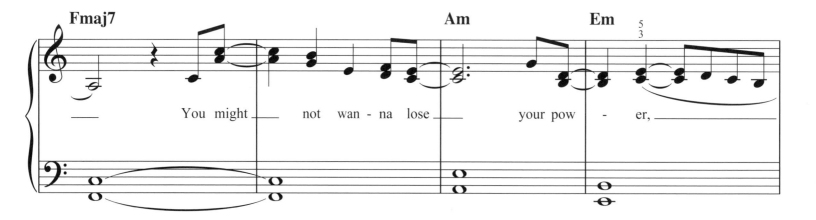

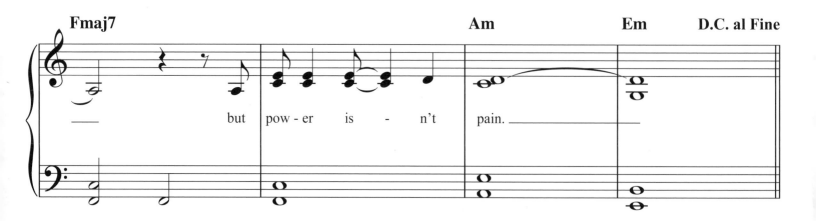